Workbook 3

Tim Falla Paul A Davies
Jane Hudson

UNIVERSITY PRESS

Great Clarendon Street, Oxford OX2 6DP

Oxford University Press is a department of the University of Oxford. It furthers the University's objective of excellence in research, scholarship, and education by publishing worldwide in

Oxford New York

Auckland Cape Town Dar es Salaam Hong Kong Karachi Kuala Lumpur Madrid Melbourne Mexico City Nairobi New Delhi Shanghai Taipei Toronto

With offices in

Argentina Austria Brazil Chile Czech Republic France Greece Guatemala Hungary Italy Japan Poland Portugal Singapore South Korea Switzerland Thailand Turkey Ukraine Vietnam

OXFORD and OXFORD ENGLISH are registered trade marks of Oxford University Press in the UK and in certain other countries

First published 2010
2014 2013 2012 2011 2010
10 9 8 7 6 5 4 3 2 1

ISBN: 978 0 19 445309 7 WORKBOOK
ISBN: 978 0 19 445326 4 STUDENT'S CD-ROM
ISBN: 978 0 19 445325 7 PACK

Printed in China

This book is printed on paper from certified and well-managed sources.

ACKNOWLEDGEMENTS

The publisher would like to thank the following for their kind permission to reproduce photographs and other copyright material: Alamy Images pp.4 (RFID transponder/Uli Nusko), 7 (woman/Picturebank), 19 (breakdown/Brian Harris), 22 (plumber/Peter Mumford), 22 (Babette Cole/Kathy deWitt), 25 (camp/Alt-6), 27 (Cumbria/Clearview), 30 (Fernando Alonso/Crash Media Group), 32 (Andy Murray/Victor Fraile), 40 (young woman/Jennie Hart), 43 (woman on laptop/Rob Wilkinson), 49 (bungee jumping/Emil Pozar), 51 (lady knitting/Tetra Images), 63 (station/The Photolibrary Wales), 73 (hotel/niceartphoto), 75 (cash machine/ICP-UK), 78 (*The Umbrellas*: Pierre August Renoir (1841-1919) French painter. Oil on canvas/World History Archive), 79 (theatre/Vehbi Koca), 81 (street/Nick Hawkes), 83 (orchestra/Paul Doyle), 83 (dancers/Roger Bamber), 86 (crop circle/John Henshall), 87 (airplane/DBurke); Corbis pp.24 (Nelson Mandela/Jon Hrusa/epa), 24 (Rigoberta Menchu/Micheline Pelletier/Sygma), 62 (Pele/Hulton-Deutsch Collection), 65 (Qingdao Bay/Liu Liqun), 78 (*Malmesbury Market* by H.C. Bryant/Fine Art Photographic Library), 81 (World War 1 Destruction in Ypres/Bettmann), 83 (*The Enamelled Saucepan* by Pablo Picasso/The Gallery Collection), 83 (Actor Nigel Hawthorne in Shakespeare's *King Lear*/Robbie Jack), 84 (Carefree woman/Roy Botterell), 84 (Woman taking photograph/Jutta Klee), 84 (Young man on street/Roy Botterell/zefa); Getty Images pp.7 (Man sitting in garden/Johner), 7 (Teen boy/Mistik PIctures), 76 (Marine life artist Wyland/AFP), 81 (Grandfather in toy business/Jose Luis Pelaez/Iconica); iStockphoto p.7 (school girl/Lesley Lister); Mike Gunnill p.12 (Piano-man/© Mike Gunnill 2010); Monty Rand p.20 (Linda Greenlaw); Oxford University Press pp.7 (Teen with mobile), 8 (Beach/Photodisc), 22 (Mountain hikers/Digital Vision), 40 (Man in velvet jacket/Image Source), 46 (Eiffel Tower/Image Source), 54 (Portrait of man/Digital Vision), 72 (Senior man/Photodisc), 81 (Family in park/Photodisc), 85 (Fast food/Photodisc); Photolibrary pp.6 (Teens celebrating soccer match/OJO Images), 7 (Man holding laptop/Rubberball), 11 (CCTV camera/Image Source), 52 (Computer class/MBI Ltd/Stockbroker), 55 (Portrait of teen girl/Brand X Pictures), 63 (Busy airport terminal/MIXA); PunchStock pp.54 (Portrait Of Young African American Man/Photodisc), 54 (Man smiling/Westend61), 54 (Young man looking away/Westend61), 55 (Teen girl with glasses/Photodisc); Rex Features pp.28 (*Super Size Me* documentary), 36 (*Wall-E* film/c. BuenaVist/Everett), 68 (Ben Way on *Secret Milionaire*/Justin Williams); Ronald Grant Archive p.44 (*The Great Imposter* film poster/Universal International Pictures (UI)); Still Pictures p.60 (Aurélien Brulé/Chanee/Biosphoto/Ruoso Cyril/BIOSphoto); Wikipedia p.35 (Alberto Coto Garcia, under Free Art Licence);

Illustrations by: Paul Daviz pp.14, 15, 16, 38, 48, 56, 64, 80; Dylan Gibson pp.31, 47.

1 On camera

READING

Before reading: Surveillance

1 Complete the sentences with the words in the box.

cash machine citizens ~~deter~~ illegal monitor password shoplifters tag warn

1 CCTV cameras are intended to *deter* people from committing crime.
2 Don't cut the ____________ off that jacket until you've tried it on.
3 It's ____________ to travel by car without a seatbelt.
4 The school has CCTV cameras to ____________ the entrances and exits.
5 I've forgotten my ____________ again!
6 I tried to ____________ her but it was too late.
7 The shop employs store detectives to catch ____________.
8 He was robbed while he was taking money out of the ____________.
9 Some British ____________ who live abroad can vote in an election.

2 Read the text. Match the sentences (1–6) with the spaces (A–E). There is one sentence you do not need.

1 So what exactly is an RFID tag?
2 In the future, consumers will be able to pay for their purchases without taking them out of the trolley.
3 At all times the management knows how many products are on the shelf and when to order more.
4 You mean you hadn't noticed?
5 As with all new technology, RFID has two sides.
6 Imagine how much easier it will be to trace a lost suitcase or to find the family cat if it has an RFID tag.

The RFID revolution

The RFID revolution has started and our lives are changing forever! **A** ________ Well, for your information, Radio Frequency Identification has been with us since the Second World War, when it was used to identify planes from a distance. Now the United States Army uses it to control its tanks in Iraq.

But RFID isn't only limited to military use. The retail giant Wal-Mart uses it to track goods from the minute they enter the warehouse to the time the customer takes them home and consumes them. **B** ________

And it's not only the retailer who can benefit from RFID technology. **C** ________ And we will be able to find out all we need to know about a product from the RFID tag on it. We will also be able to do our weekly shopping without actually having to enter a supermarket.

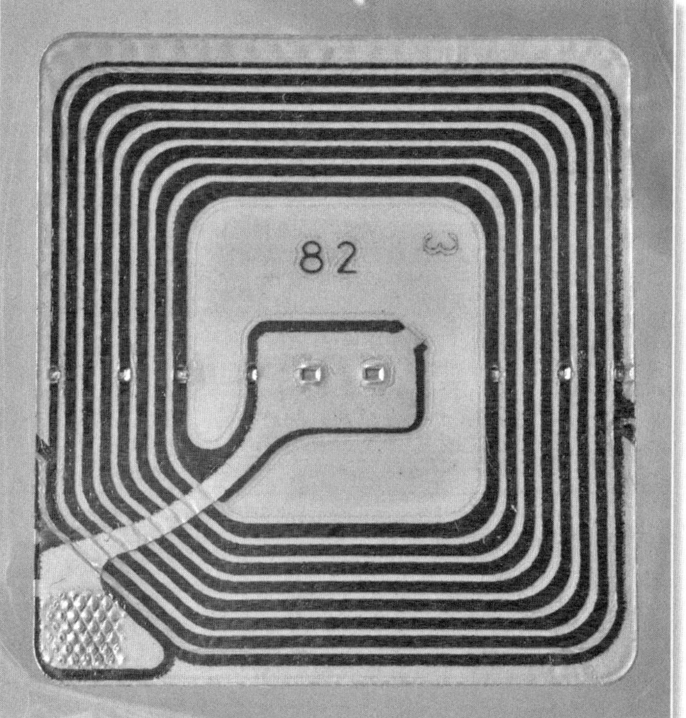

D ________ It's an electronic label formed by a small antenna and a chip the size of a grain of sand. The great advantage of RFID technology is that the tags can be read from a distance and do not have to be in the visual field of a laser reader.

Other uses of this revolutionary idea run from pet identification to luggage labelling in airports. **E** ________

But the personal information on the tag poses a threat to security, and there is a growing group of opponents to RFID.

Whatever happens, you can be sure that RFID is here to stay. Once it is fully implemented our lives will never be the same again.

VOCABULARY

Somebody is watching you

1 Replace the words in bold with a synonym.

cash machine citizens deter illegal initially interact monitoring offenders ~~potential~~ shoplifters surveillance tags vulnerable warned work out

1 Wearing a seatbelt can prevent a **possible** disaster in a car crash. potential.
2 My neighbours have bought a dog to **stop** burglars from breaking into their house. ________
3 **Being watched** is something we're all having to get used to. ________
4 The **people** of London are protesting about the increase in knife crime. ________
5 **At first** we were going to stay in a hotel, but then we decided to go camping. ________
6 They were interested to see how the cat would **behave** with their two dogs. ________
7 Nobody **told** me in **advance** about the road works. ________
8 The bank was shut so he took some money out of the **place outside the bank**. ________
9 Driving without a licence is **not allowed by law**. ________
10 Old people and small children are left quite **weak** after suffering from the illness. ________
11 That store has installed new security cameras to catch **thieves**. ________
12 The new centre for young **criminals** is going to open next week. ________
13 She had to ask the price because the clothes had no **labels**. ________
14 They're **watching** all the employees to find out who is using the office phone for personal calls. ________
15 He couldn't **solve** the Maths problem. ________

Word formations: nouns

2 Complete the sentences with the noun form of the verb in brackets.

1 Astronauts are very excited about a new development in space technology. (develop)
2 My mother has always taken great care over her ________. (appear)
3 I had to send the email again because I had fogotten to include the ________. (attach)
4 When the company rang the man four times in one day, he complained of ________. (harrass)
5 They were very disappointed at the ________ they received at the meeting. (treat)
6 Experts are carrying out an ________ into what caused the accident. (investigate)
7 There was no ________ of her efforts. (recognize)
8 The famous actor tried to avoid ________ by wearing a disguise. (detect)

Verbs for looking

3 Match the two parts of the sentences.

1 The little boy **gaped**	a a friend at the supermarket.
2 The teacher **glanced**	b at me for a long time.
3 The old man **glared**	c into the dark room.
4 The police carefully **observed**	d over the fence.
5 My nosy neighbour **peeked**	e the people entering the bank.
6 My grandfather **peered**	f angrily at the naughty children.
7 I suddenly **spotted**	g at his new bike in surprise.
8 The child **stared**	h quickly at her watch.

4 Complete the sentences with the verbs in bold from exercise 3.

1 We all stood and gaped in astonishment when our teacher came into school in a brand new sports car.
2 We ________ our aunt at the station before she saw us.
3 Our neighbour ________ over the high wall and asked us why we were making so much noise.
4 The girl carefully ________ how her mother was cooking the dish before trying it herself.
5 She was so surprised at how tall her cousin had grown that she just stood in the doorway and ________ at him.
6 The taxi driver ________ at the man when he said he had no money to pay the fare.
7 The little boys ________ into their grandmother's bag to see if they could find some sweets.
8 The children were very quiet and so she ________ into the room to see what they were doing.

Present tense contrast

1 **Choose the correct alternatives.**

1 The match (starts) / **'s starting** at 8.30 p.m.
2 We **go** / **'re going** tonight.
3 He **drives** / **'s driving** an elegant black Mercedes to work every day.
4 Listen! Kim **sings** / **'s singing** in the shower again!
5 They **get up** / **'re getting up** early every day.
6 You **always leave** / **'re always leaving** your dirty socks on the floor!

2 **Match the uses of the present tenses with the sentences (1–6) in exercise 1.**

Present simple

a For habits and routines ____
b For a permanent situation or fact ____
c For timetables and schedules 1____

Present continuous

d For something happening now or about now ____
e For describing annoying habits (with *always*) ____
f For arrangements in the future ____

3 **Complete the sentences with the correct form of the verbs in the box.**

~~do~~ get go go out have open play snow

1 I 'm doing a project on global warming.
2 They ____________ to school in the town centre.
3 The new sports shop ____________ at 9 a.m. tomorrow.
4 We ____________ lunch really late on Sundays.
5 They ____________ always ____________ loud music. I hate it!
6 She ____________ with her friends tonight.
7 He ____________ home at about 7.30 p.m.
8 Look! It ____________!

4 **Rewrite the sentences correctly.**

1 We're believing in freedom of speech.
We believe in freedom of speech.
2 They're liking eating ice cream in the summer.
____
3 I'm preferring fish to meat.
____
4 He's needing a new coat.
____
5 I'm wanting to have a drink of water.
____
6 We're hating walking to school in the rain.
____

5 **Use the words to write questions in the present simple or the present continuous.**

1 you / like / playing football?
Do you like playing football?
2 she / want / to go / home now?
____
3 what / you / listen to / at the moment?
____
4 they / prefer / the cinema or the theatre?
____
5 he / need / a glass of water?
____
6 you / enjoy / this play?
____
7 she / go / home now?
____
8 this jacket / belong / to you?
____

CHALLENGE!

Write sentences to describe

1 two things you do every day:
____
2 two annoying things people in your family do:
____
3 your school's starting and finishing times:
____
4 two arrangements you've made for the future:
____

Cultural dress

1 Solve the anagrams to find items of clothing.

1 sesrd dress
2 ncitu ______
3 cohonp ______
4 sira ______
5 dasafrehc ______
6 lsasdna ______
7 buntar ______
8 apkra ______
9 moknio ______
10 sotob ______

2 Complete the mind map with words from the box.

~~ankle-length~~ ~~baggy~~ checked ~~cotton~~ decorated ~~fine~~ fur hard knee-length linen long long-sleeved loose matching patterned ~~plain~~ seal skin short-sleeved soft stripy strong thick tight wide wooden

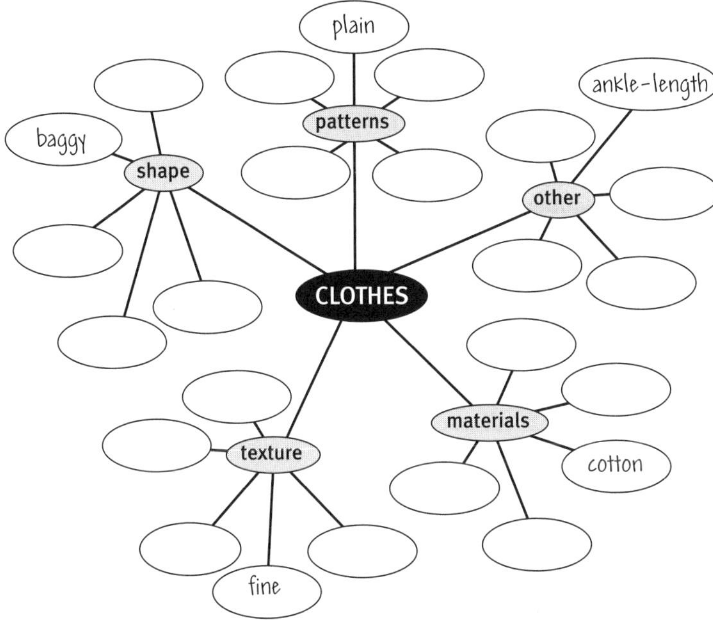

3 Rewrite the sentences that are incorrect.

1 It's a yellow smart tunic.
It's a smart yellow tunic.
2 They're linen loose trousers.
______
3 It's a green tight kimono.
______
4 They're cotton baggy shorts.
______
5 They're strong seal skin boots.
______
6 It's a fur warm coat.
______
7 It's a checked wide skirt.
______
8 They're patterned knee-length socks.
______

4 Describe the pictures using two adjectives from A and a noun from B.

A baggy checked fur knee-length ~~linen~~ long-sleeved ~~loose~~ patterned plain plain short-sleeved stripy

B ~~suit~~ skirt shirt trousers T-shirt hat

1 He's wearing a loose linen suit.

4 ______

2 ______

5 ______

3 ______

6 ______

CHALLENGE!

Write about the clothes you wear:

at home: ______

to play sport: ______

to go to school: ______

Verb patterns: verb + infinitive / verb + *-ing* form

1 Choose the correct alternatives.

1 I fancy **to go out** / **going out** for a pizza, don't you?
2 If you happen **to see** / **seeing** Kerry, tell her I called.
3 Do you want **to watch** / **watching** a film tonight?
4 We managed **to finish** / **finishing** our homework quickly.
5 I can't help **to laugh** / **laughing** when someone falls over.
6 We hope **to go** / **going** to the Mediterranean this year.
7 They refused **to help** / **helping** us with the project.
8 I meant **to phone** / **phoning** you last night but I forgot.

2 Complete the dialogue with the infinitive or *-ing* form of the verbs in brackets.

A I'm fed up! I spent all last night [1] studying (study) for today's exam.
B Did you manage [2] ______ (learn) it all?
A More or less. But I can't face [3] ______ (do) the same again tonight.
B No, I don't enjoy [4] ______ (study) either, but we've nearly finished.
A I feel like [5] ______ (go out) for a change. We've been studying for weeks.
B Well, there's no way we can avoid [6] ______ (take) exams. Let's plan a trip for when we finish.
A That's a good idea! Where do you suggest [7] ______ (go)?
B I fancy [8] ______ (lie) on a beach somewhere doing absolutely nothing.
A Excellent idea. Let's do it!

3 Choose the correct alternatives.

1 I forgot **to lock** / **locking** the car yesterday so someone stole the radio.
2 I'll never forget **to go** / **going** horse riding when I was little. I was terrified!
3 He stopped **to buy** / **buying** a newspaper on the way home, but there weren't any left.
4 I remember **to put** / **putting** my keys in my pocket, but now I can't find them!
5 We tried **to find** / **finding** a cheap flight, but we were too late.
6 After university she went on **to become** / **becoming** a brain surgeon.

4 Complete the sentences with the infinitive or the *-ing* form of the verbs in the box.

eat drink learn post push ~~say~~ visit

1 I remembered to say ______ 'Happy Birthday' to Sarah. Did you?
2 She stopped ______ coffee so she would sleep better.
3 I forgot ______ that letter. Sorry!
4 His car won't start, so we're going to try ______ it.
5 They went on ______ in the restaurant all night.
6 Do you remember ______ your grandparents when you were little?
7 My brother tried ______ Japanese at night school, but he gave up after two months.

CHALLENGE!

Write a sentence about something:

you remember doing when you were little.

______

you've tried to do recently but couldn't.

______

you forgot to do recently.

______

A letter to an exchange student

Preparation

1 Match the two halves of the set expressions.

1 Anyway, that's — d
2 I'll tell you a bit
3 I'm really looking
4 May I
5 Do write soon and
6 I'm enclosing

a introduce myself?
b a photo of me and my friends.
c about my family.
d all for now.
e tell me all about your country.
f forward to visiting you.

2 Complete the letter with the expressions from exercise 1.

Dear . . .

1 ______________________ I'm Cathy Lord, your new exchange student. I'm eighteen years old, and I live with my parents and my brothers in Manchester, a town in the north of England. Have you heard of it?

2 ______________________ I'm the girl in the spotty T-shirt in the foreground and the guy on the left is my brother, Stewart. The girl in the white leggings is my best friend, Sandy. She's really nice, and I'm sure you'll like her too.

3 ______________________ My parents are both teachers, but luckily they don't teach at my school! My brother Stewart in the photo is seventeen and he's a lot of fun. My other brother, Frank, is only twelve, so he's a bit of a pain.

4 ______________________
5 ______________________

Do you go out with your friends at the weekend? What kind of music do you like?

6 ______________________

Best wishes,

Cathy

3 Tick (✓) the topics of the paragraphs in Cathy's letter. There are three topics you do not need.

1 Introduction and general personal details ☐
2 Sports, hobbies and interests ☐
3 Describing a photo of your friends ☐
4 School ☐
5 Describing your own country and its people ☐
6 Describing your family ☐
7 Asking for information about the other person ☐

4 Put the words in the correct order to make questions.

1 you / town centre / the / Do / in / live
______________________?
2 your / like / What's / school
______________________?
3 you / your / do / What / in / do / free time
______________________?
4 you / cousin / got / a / Have
______________________?
5 kind / do / What / of / you / music / like
______________________?
6 your / school / What's / subject / best / at
______________________?

Writing task

5 In your notebook write a letter of introduction to Cathy. Use the Writing Bank on page 90 to help you. Write 150–200 words and include this information:

- some facts about yourself
- two paragraphs, each about a topic from exercise 3
- some questions asking for information about Cathy.

Check your work

Have you

☐ started and finished your letter appropriately?
☐ organized your letter into four paragraphs?
☐ written 150–200 words?
☐ checked grammar, spelling and punctuation?

SELF CHECK 1: GRAMMAR

1 Complete each pair of sentences with the present simple and the present continuous forms of the verb.

1 drive

a My father ________ to work every day.

b He can't talk now. He ________.

2 play

a How often ________ you ________ tennis?

b ________ you ________ tennis next weekend?

3 not speak

a My mother ________ English.

b She's upset because her friend ________ to her.

4 shout

a ________ your teacher ever ________?

b Why ________ that man ________?

5 not go

a We ________ to school on Saturdays.

b We ________ to school tomorrow because it's the first day of the holidays.

6 always take

a I'm fed up with my sister. She ________ my CDs without asking.

b She ________ a lot of photos when she's on holiday.

Your score /12

2 Complete the sentences with the correct form of the verb in the box.

> not believe belong come cry not understand not wear not work want

1 I'm sorry, I ________. Can you say that again?

2 What's the matter? Why ________ you ________?

3 My brother ________ a motorbike for his birthday.

4 Run! The bus ________.

5 The children are cold because they ________ coats.

6 I ________ he can run that fast. It's impossible.

7 ________ that car ________ to you?

8 The washing machine is on but it ________.

Your score /8

3 Complete the sentences with the present simple form of the verbs in the box and the infinitive or *-ing* form of the verbs in brackets.

> avoid can't face enjoy expect fail feel like manage promise refuse suggest

1 When you visit a hot country, you should ________ directly in the sun. (sit)

2 I don't know how my mother ________ six children and go out to work. (look after)

3 They ________ dinner for their friends – it's fun! (make)

4 We're sorry. We ________ late again. (not be)

5 It's a beautiful day. I ________ for a long walk in the park this afternoon. (go)

6 She ________ any more money to her brother until he pays her back. (lend)

7 The doctor ________ so much coffee if you want to sleep better. (not drink)

8 Olivia is so embarrased about her new haircut that she ________ the house! (leave)

9 I've studied a lot, so I ________ well in my exams next month. (do)

10 The teacher says she'll call our parents if we ________ our homework on time. (hand in)

Your score /10

4 Choose a or b to complete the sentences.

1 I still remember

a to lock the door. b breaking my leg when I was little.

2 She nearly forgot

a visiting her relatives. b to visit the dentist.

3 On the way home he stopped

a to buy a newspaper. b chatting to a friend.

4 After finishing the book, she went on

a reading until midnight. b to read the next one in the series.

5 You could try

a coming to the training sessions b to come last week.

Your score /10

Total /40

SELF CHECK 1: VOCABULARY

1 Complete the vocabulary quiz with words from Unit 1.

Quiz

1 There are several people who ________ the CCTV cameras for signs of criminal activity.

2 When the old lady needed help, a lot of people offered her their ________.

3 That material is much too ________ to wear in summer.

4 By wearing a mask, the man was able to commit crimes and avoid ________.

5 When taking money out of a ________, you should check that the person behind you isn't too close.

6 The woman looked so strange that it was difficult not to ________ at her.

7 Cotton or ________ are good materials to wear in summer.

8 You need to wear a ________ shirt in the evening here.

9 She was dressed all in red: a red skirt and ________ jacket.

10 This coat is ________, so it will keep you very warm.

11 I prefer wearing plain colours, so I never buy ________ clothes.

12 From his position, the security guard was able to ________ the shoppers without being seen.

13 A person's ________ can raise suspicion, for example, wearing a long coat on a warm day.

14 ________ often claim that they simply forgot to pay for the items they are hiding under their coat.

15 Wearing ________ clothes will keep you cool, as they allow the air to circulate.

16 The security guards use walkie-talkies so that they can ________ with each other.

17 There are lots of ________ blouses in the shops, but it's still too cold to wear them.

18 Another word for *loose* is ________ when we talk about clothes.

19 'The hospital was fantastic. I can't complain about the ________ I received.'

20 To ________ at somebody means to stare angrily at them.

Your score /20

2 Complete the text with the correct words (a–d).

Caught on CCTV

A man who campaigned for CCTV cameras to be [1]________ near his flat has been convicted of vandalism – after being caught on the same CCTV cameras which he had asked for. Liam Jordan had [2]________ to the police of repeated acts of vandalism near his flat in Leeds. He claimed the CCTV cameras would [3]________ potential vandals. When police were [4]________ the new CCTV cameras, they were amazed to see Mr Jordan coming out of his flat, picking up a brick and throwing it through a neighbour's window. He was then seen running back into his flat, not knowing that he was being [5]________. Mr Jordan then [6]________ the police himself and told them that vandals had broken his neighbour's window! In court, Mr Jordan said he hadn't [7]________ that the CCTV cameras had [8]________ been installed, and that he broke the window in order to draw attention to the problems of vandalism in the area. He was [9]________ to pay £560 compensation for the [10]________ to the window.

	a	b	c	d
1	a installed	b inserted	c taken	d initialled
2	a reclaimed	b said	c told	d complained
3	a avoid	b deter	c warn	d offend
4	a working out	b staring	c looking	d monitoring
5	a stared	b watched	c looked	d seen
6	a interacted	b contacted	c reported	d spoken
7	a realized	b recognized	c found	d revealed
8	a initially	b yet	c already	d illegally
9	a ordered	b tagged	c reported	d convicted
10	a hurt	b damage	c harm	d injury

Your score /10

Total /30

2 Memories

READING

Before reading: Abilities

1 Complete the sentences with the words in the box.

aptitude ~~artistic~~ baffled genius good at proficient skills

1 His interests are more artistic ______ than technical.
2 Even the experts were ______ by the symptoms.
3 As a child, he had a great ______ for music and he could play four instruments, including the piano, by the age of 8.
4 Have you always been ______ maths?
5 She has fantastic communication ______.
6 He's very bright, but he isn't exactly a ______.
7 For this job, you need to be ______ in several languages.

2 Choose the correct preposition.

1 She's scared **at** / **of** heights.
2 She's proficient **in** / **about** French, but her Spanish is quite rusty.
3 I'm not very good **about** / **at** maths or science.
4 Those children aren't interested **in** / **at** learning.
5 We're all baffled **by** / **for** this problem.

3 Read the text. Match the headings (1–6) with the paragraphs (A–E). There is one heading that you do not need.

1 Patient provides the answer
2 International orchestras collaborate
3 Mystery solved and Piano Man named
4 Doctors make the music connection
5 Public help not useful
6 Strange man found on beach

4 Are the sentences true or false? Write T or F.

1 The unidentified man was found by a road. ____
2 When hospital staff gave him a pencil and some paper, he drew a picture of a piano. ____
3 The Piano Man was able to understand the Norwegian ship's captain. ____
4 The French embassy contacted his parents. ____
5 The man is now recovering from his illness in hospital. ____

The Piano Man

A ______

At midnight on April 7th, 2006, an unidentified man was picked up on a beach on the coast of Britain by police. He was wearing a black jacket, smart trousers and a tie, all of which were extremely wet. He was acting very nervously and he refused to speak to the police. They took him to a hospital nearby, where the doctors could find nothing wrong with him.

B ______

So who was this man, and where did he come from? The only clue to his identity came when he was given a pencil and a piece of paper and he drew a beautiful picture of a grand piano. When hospital staff excitedly took him to a piano, they were surprised at how well he played. From then on the patient became known as the Piano Man, and the National Missing Persons Helpline published a phone number in the hope that someone would come forward to identify him.

C ______

Calls came in from all over the world from people recognizing him as a French street musician or a Czech concert pianist. The Piano Man didn't seem to understand any of the language experts the police brought in – they even tried a Norwegian ship's captain to see if the Piano Man understood Norwegian. However, his identity remained a mystery and the search went on.

D ______

The end of the story of the Piano Man is, in fact, a bit of an anticlimax. One Friday in August he woke up and told a doctor he was German. The hospital got in touch with the German embassy at once, and they in turn contacted his parents, who confirmed his identity.

E ______

So, it turned out that the Piano Man was, in fact, Andreas Grassi, aged twenty, from Prosdorf, Germany, who was suffering from a serious mental illness when police found him on that beach. He's now recovering from his illness at home while the publicity his story created dies down.

VOCABULARY

Unknown white male

1 Complete the sentences with the words in the box.

at once baffled cope discharge enrol escorted flip-flops outgoing patchy portrayed ~~rucksack~~ scrawled severity skull stunning

1 When I go travelling, I'm going to take a rucksack instead of a suitcase.
2 Everybody was ________ by the new registration procedure.
3 The x-ray showed a crack in her ________ from where she'd banged her head.
4 Kate doesn't know anything about history, and her knowledge of geography is very ________.
5 The view from the window of our hotel room was ________. It took your breath away.
6 I can't ________ with all my work at the moment. I need some help.
7 An ambulance arrived and took the victim to hospital ________.
8 They didn't realize the ________ of his illness until he collapsed.
9 When are they going to ________ your grandfather from hospital?
10 Two police officers ________ the criminal into court.
11 Tim is going to ________ in a business school next year.
12 The little boy ________ his name onto the front of his book.
13 My sister is very ________ and so she has a lot of friends.
14 She put on her ________ and went down to the beach.
15 In the novel, the main character was ________ as a very nervous individual.

Adjectives + propositions

2 Complete the sentences with the right prepositions.

1 I'm scared of spiders.
2 They're happy ________ their new house.
3 My sister's upset ________ the argument she had this morning.
4 We're bored ________ this game. Let's play something else.
5 Ryan's nervous ________ his first driving lesson.
6 They were surprised ________ the takeover of the factory.
7 Sarah was ashamed ________ her behaviour the day before.
8 I'm worried ________ my mother.
9 I think Suzy was always jealous ________ her younger sister.
10 My parents are very proud ________ all their children.

Phrasal verbs

3 Circle the correct particles in the sentences.

1 We set **off** / **on** / **up** / **in** as soon as everybody was ready.
2 He woke **down** / **out** / **on** / **up** when he heard his alarm.
3 Our plans to go camping fell **out** / **back** / **through** / **in** because of the bad weather.
4 They were all late because the bus broke **in** / **up** / **down** / **out**.
5 I'm really looking forward to going **out** / **in** / **off** / **on** tonight.
6 'Hold **up** / **down** / **on** / **out** and I'll make some coffee.'
7 We came **back** / **through** / **on** / **off** at midnight.
8 They stayed **off** / **up** / **down** / **in** because it was raining.

Phrasal verbs with *up*

4 Rewrite the sentences with a phrasal verb formed by the verbs in the box and the particle *up*.

get give go grow speak stand ~~tidy~~ turn

1 My mother is always **cleaning**.
My mother is always tidying up.
2 When he **becomes an adult**, he wants to be a firefighter.
____
3 They **got to their feet** in order to see better.
____
4 Hardly anyone **arrived** at the meeting.
____
5 We usually **get out of bed** late at the weekend.
____
6 If you find the lessons difficult, you shouldn't **stop trying**.
____
7 Sales figures **increased** by 5% last month.
____
8 People can't hear you if you don't **talk louder**.
____

Past tense contrast

1 Rewrite the sentences that are incorrect.

1 Did you went to school yesterday?
Did you go to school yesterday?

2 I hadn't breakfast this morning.

3 You was singing in the shower!

4 Was drawing Mark a picture when the teacher walked in?

5 They weren't wear caps.

6 Had you read the book before you saw the film?

7 She was angry because he'd forgot her birthday.

8 We drived to Italy for our holiday last year.

2 Choose the correct alternatives.

1 I **got up** / **was getting up** / **had got up** at 7 o'clock today.
2 It was really hot and the sun **shone** / **was shining** / **had shone**.
3 A dog ran onto the pitch while they **played** / **were playing** / **had played** football.
4 I saw you yesterday in the police station. What **did you do** / **were you doing** / **had you done** there?
5 I couldn't open the door because I **forgot** / **was forgetting** / **'d forgotten** my keys.
6 She **didn't go** / **wasn't going** / **hadn't gone** to the doctor's because she forgot her appointment.
7 The house was quiet because everybody **went** / **was going** / **had gone** out.
8 **Did you buy** / **Were you buying** / **Had you bought** that top in the sales?

3 Change the sentences from affirmative to negative or from negative to affirmative.

1 She had dinner and she went to bed.
She didn't have dinner and she didn't go to bed.

2 It wasn't raining, so we went out.

3 I hadn't brought a sandwich, so I didn't have lunch.

4 They were nervous because they had an exam.

5 The teacher was angry because the class wasn't working.

6 They weren't happy because they didn't have tickets to the theme park.

7 She'd brought her swimming costume, so she went swimming.

4 Complete the story with a suitable past tense form of the verbs in brackets.

When I was little, my dad [1] brought (bring) me home a goldfish. I was delighted, but something soon went wrong. My parents [2] ______ (talk) to some friends who had come to visit us, and I was a bit bored, so I [3] ______ (go) into the kitchen to see my goldfish. The packet of goldfish food [4] ______ (stand) on the table next to the goldfish bowl and I picked it up to look at it. My parents [5] ______ (tell) me never to feed the goldfish, but I [6] ______ (think) it looked a bit hungry, so I [7] ______ (decide) to feed it. Unfortunately, the lid came off the packet of goldfish food, and the entire contents [8] ______ (fall) into the water. I was really embarrassed and I felt incredibly guilty because I [9] ______ (be) so disobedient. I [10] ______ (run) into the living room crying and eventually I told my parents what [11] ______ (happen). My goldfish survived, though, and went on to live for another two years!

CHALLENGE!

Use the questions to write about your favourite childhood memory.
Where were you?
What were you doing?
What happened?

How did you feel?

1 Match the pictures (A–H) with the sentences (1–8).

1 I lost my expensive watch. E
2 I went to France on my own. I really missed my friends back home. ___
3 My jeans tore when I sat down in class. ___
4 I shouted at my little sister and I made her cry. ___
5 I waited an hour to see the doctor yesterday! ___
6 I had my end-of-course exam last week. ___
7 I went to the dentist this morning. ___
8 My brother got a TV for his birthday. ___

2 Complete the sentences with the *-ed* or *-ing* form of the verbs in brackets.

1 That film's really amusing (amuse). I laughed all the way through it.
2 I forgot it was my sister's birthday. I'm ________ (embarass).
3 That maths question was really ________ (confuse). I didn't understand it at all.
4 He's ________ (delight). He passed his driving test this morning.
5 They managed to get tickets for the match tonight. They're very ________ (relieve).
6 The weather's really ________ (depress). It's raining today and it rained yesterday, too.
7 He was very ________ (disappoint) when his grandmother didn't give him a birthday present.
8 She's really ________ (please) with her new laptop.

3 Complete the puzzle by forming nouns from the adjectives. Use the suffixes *-ment*, *-ness* or *-ion*. Write your own answers vertically and find the mystery word in the grey boxes.

1 homesick	4 disappointed	7 excited
2 embarrassed	5 irritated	8 sad
3 depressed	6 confused	9 frustrated

1 HOMESICKNESS

Mystery word: ________

CHALLENGE!

Answer the questions with at least two adjectives.

How did you feel:

the last time you were away from home for a few days?

____

when you sat your last exam?

____

the last time you spoke to someone you didn't know?

____

GRAMMAR

used to

1 Put the words in the correct order to make sentences and questions.

1 used / lazy / he / be / very / to
He used to be very lazy.
2 you / motorbike / to / did / have / use / a
_______________?
3 didn't / be / she / to / so / bad-tempered / use
_______________.
4 live / village / use / didn't / in / a / they / to
_______________.
5 to / a / there / in / used / cinema / that / be / street
_______________.
6 school / she / a / to / did / go / to / use / different
_______________?

2 Rewrite the sentences that are incorrect.

1 I use to live in the country, but now I don't.
I used to live in the country, but now I don't.
2 Did you used to wear glasses?
3 They didn't use to do any homework.
4 He uses to have a motorbike.
5 We used to play in the park when we were little.
6 She used cried a lot when she was a baby.

3 Use the words to write questions to ask about someone's childhood.

1 What / wear?
What did you use to wear?
2 What time / go to bed?
3 Who / play with?
4 Where / go on holiday?
5 What / watch on TV?
6 What / hate eating?
7 Which school / go to?

4 Now answer the questions in exercise 3.

1 _______________
2 _______________
3 _______________
4 _______________
5 _______________
6 _______________
7 _______________

5 Look at the picture. Complete the sentences comparing Gary at the age of 17 and Gary at 41, using *used to*.

1 Gary used to have a motorbike, but now he has a car. (have)
2 He _______ thin, but now he _______ quite fat. (be)
3 He _______ glasses, but now he doesn't. (wear)
4 He _______ a suit, but now he does. (not wear)
5 He _______ long hair, but now he _______ short hair. (have)
6 He _______ his friends every day, but now he _______ them at the weekend. (see)
7 He _______ a laptop, but now he does. (not carry)
8 He _______ to school, but now he _______ to work! (go)

CHALLENGE!

How were you different when you were little? What did you use to do that you don't do now? Write three sentences.

1 _______________
2 _______________
3 _______________

Notes

Preparation

1 **Match the two halves of the phrasal verbs in boxes A and B to complete the definitions below.**

A
~~look~~ pick run out put call look
look forward lock

B
to back ~~after~~ for of up up away

1 care for *look after*
2 tidy ____
3 phone someone who has called you ____
4 collect ____
5 search for ____
6 not have any more of ____
7 keep safe somewhere by using a key ____
8 anticipate with pleasure ____

2 **Complete the following notes with the phrasal verbs from exercise 1.**

Paul,
I'll be late back tonight, so could you please [1] look after Rex? I usually feed him at about 7 o'clock. We've [2] ____ dog food, I'm afraid, could you [3] ____ some MisterDog from the supermarket? Don't forget to [4] ____ the food in the cupboard afterwards. He'll eat the whole packet, otherwise!
Thanks – I know it's a lot to ask.
Marie

Amy,
Molly came round just after you left. Did she leave her watch here last time? She's [5] ____ it everywhere at home. She'll be out most of the day, but you can [6] ____ any time after six o'clock.
Mum

3 **Rewrite each pair of sentences as one sentence, linked with one of the conjunctions in the box. In some sentences more than one answer is possible.**

because but even though since so though
whereas while

1 I didn't want to go to the party. I was tired.
I didn't want to go to the party because I was tired.
2 They didn't like the food. They didn't say anything about it.
____
3 We enjoyed the film. We went to see it again.
____
4 Karen is a vegetarian. I eat a lot of meat.
____
5 They recommended the hotel. They hadn't enjoyed their stay.
____
6 We stayed in and played cards. We were too late to see the film.
____

Writing task

4 **Imagine that you had to go away for a day or two. In your notebook write a last minute message to your best friend. Write 50–60 words and use conjunctions where possible. Include this information:**

- tell him/her where you've gone and why
- remind him/her to do something
- ask him/her to buy something
- say when you'll be back.

Check your work

Have you

- [ ] written 50-60 words?
- [ ] included all the information?
- [ ] used conjunctions where possible?
- [ ] checked grammar, spelling and punctuation?

SELF CHECK 2: GRAMMAR

1 Use the words to write past simple and past continuous sentences. There is sometimes more than one correct answer.

1 when / I / get home / I have dinner

____

2 the sun / shine / and / people / swim in the lake

____

3 My brother / drop / a plate / while / he / lay / the table

____

4 Lily / finish / her homework / before / she / go out

____

5 When / we / drive / to the airport / we / see / an accident

____

6 Her parents / wait / for her / when / she / come home

____

7 The boys / break / a window / when / they / play / football

____

8 it / rain / hard / and / the waves / crash / on the beach

____

9 Who / you / talk / to / when / I / met / you / ?

____

10 While / everyone / celebrate / Joe's birthday / someone / break into / the house

____

Your score ___ **/10**

2 Complete the sentences with the past simple and past perfect forms of the verbs in brackets. In each sentence you will need to use both tenses.

1 After the children _________ their homework, they _________ TV. (do, watch)

2 Amy _________ because she _________ the question. (not answer, not hear)

3 My father _________ a busy day so he _________ to bed early. (have, go)

4 We _________ a reminder because we _________ the phone bill. (receive, not pay)

5 After my sister _________ her clothes, she _________ them _________. (iron, put away)

6 Adrian _________ something strange and so he _________ ill. (eat, be)

Your score ___ **/12**

3 Complete the dialogue with the affirmative, negative or interrogative form of *used to* and the verbs in brackets.

A What did you do before you became a writer?

B I was a waiter. I [1] _________ in a restaurant in the centre of town. (work)

A Was your life very different then?

B Yes, it was. I [2] _________ very early to open the restaurant. (get up)

A What time [3] _________ you _________ the restaurant to go home? (leave)

B Most days I [4] _________ work until about midnight. (not finish)

A What [5] _________ you _________ in your free time? (do)

B Well, I [6] _________ much time for myself. (not have) But I [7] _________ to the cinema every Sunday night. (go)

A When did you decide to leave your job?

B Well, I always [8] _________ of writing my own novel, but I thought it was impossible. (dream) Then one day I bought a notebook and I went to sit in the park. That was the beginning of my new life ...

Your score ___ **/8**

4 Rewrite the sentences with *used to* where possible.

1 When I was little I cried a lot.

____

2 What did you wear when you were young?

____

3 My Dad bought me a car for my eighteenth birthday.

____

4 There was a theatre in my town.

____

5 We didn't see my grandparents much in the past.

____

6 When I was ten, we moved to a big city.

____

7 Last Monday Adam broke his leg.

____

8 I didn't like vegetables as a child.

____

9 My family didn't go camping very often.

____

10 I didn't get a single present on my last birthday.

____

Your score ___ **/10**

Total ___ **/40**

SELF CHECK 2: VOCABULARY

1 Complete the vocabulary quiz with words from Unit 2.

Quiz

1 ________ are special shoes you wear on the beach.

2 He was ________ by the road signs, which showed different ways to the town centre.

3 We couldn't finish the crossword, and so we ________ up.

4 I can't ________ with the amount of work. It really is too much for one person to do.

5 She felt ________ for making her sister cry.

6 They were upset ________ their parents' decision.

7 He takes his books to school in a ________.

8 I'm scared ________ heights.

9 It was so cold that we decided to ________ in and play computer games.

10 My brother was very ________ when he first went away to college.

11 He was ________ about the exam because he hadn't revised for it.

12 He was such a quiet person. Everyone was shocked at the ________ of the crime he'd committed.

13 She has a lot of friends because she's very ________.

14 I'm surprised ________ your results. I thought you were going to pass!

15 He told me to ________ on while he fetched his jacket.

16 I was very ________ when I found my wallet – I thought I'd lost it!!

17 When the roller coaster ride started, I was absolutely ________, but then I started to enjoy it.

18 I've forgotten many things about my childhood – my memories are ________.

19 They were ________ with the present we had bought them. They loved it!

20 My father ________ up on a farm. He lived there until he was 18.

Your score /20

2 Complete the letter with the missing prepositions.

Dear Catherine,

Thanks for your letter. It was great to hear from you. I hope your exams are over now and you're happy [1]________ the results.

I've just had an awful weekend. We had planned to go camping, but in the end all our plans fell [2]________ because of our car. Everything was fine on Saturday morning when we set [3]________, and we had no problems for the first half of our journey. Unfortunately, just before lunch, the car broke [4]________. My Dad tried several times to call for help, but the number was always engaged. In the end he gave [5]________ and we ate the picnic my Mum had packed that morning. After lunch my Dad decided to go and get help with my brother, so I stayed behind with my mother. We soon got tired [6]________ waiting, and so we fell asleep in the car. When we woke [7]________ it was getting late and my Dad and my brother had still not come [8]________. We started to get very worried [9]________ them. Just then they turned [10]________ in a van, which took our car to a garage. We went home in a taxi which had been following the van.

I hope you had a better weekend than me. Please write soon and tell me what you've been doing.

Best wishes

Millie

Your score /10

Total /30

3 Nine to five

READING

Before reading: New experiences

1 Complete the sentences with the words in the box.

break ~~embark on~~ opportunity promoted settle in struggle

1 After fifteen years as a lawyer, he decided to *embark on* a career as a journalist.
2 It can be very difficult for women to ________ into professions that are dominated by men.
3 When I was offered a job as a DJ, I was thrilled to be given the ________.
4 The first woman in the UK to become a doctor had to ________ to be recognized by other members of the profession.
5 Despite not having much experience, he was ________ quickly.
6 You'll find everything a bit new and strange at first, but I'm sure you'll ________ quickly.

2 Read the text and choose the best answer.

1 Linda is
 a American.
 b British.
 c Canadian.

2 Her first deep-sea fishing trip was
 a when she was a child.
 b before she was twenty.
 c in 1986.

3 Linda took up swordfishing because
 a she needed to earn some money.
 b all her family are fishermen.
 c she loves boats and catching fish.

4 On the boat described in *The Hungry Ocean*,
 a there were five people.
 b there were six people.
 C there were four people.

5 Linda prefers to be described as
 a a fisherwoman.
 b a fisherlady.
 c a fisherman.

Linda Greenlaw: SWORDFISH FISHERMAN

Not only does Linda Greenlaw do one of the most dangerous jobs in the world, but she also does it extremely well. She has been described as 'one of the best captains on the entire East coast' and that, in one of the leading countries in the fishing industry, is praise indeed.

Linda was born and brought up on Isle au Haut, a tiny island ten kilometres off the coast of Maine, USA. She fell in love with fishing as a child, and she worked on fishing boats during her summer breaks from college.

Her first opportunity to go on a deep-sea fishing trip came when she was nineteen. Alden Leeman, a man she'd never met before, hired her for thirty days on his swordfishing boat. The trip was a success and eventually Alden offered Linda her first boat to captain in 1986, which probably made her the only woman ever to captain a swordfishing boat.

So, why did she take up swordfishing in the first place? Linda says that not only does she like the way she feels on a boat, but she also gets passionate about catching a fish. More than anything, she's proud of being a fisherman, even more so than she is of being a best-selling author.

Linda has published four books to date, the first of which, *The Hungry Ocean*, was top of the New York bestseller list for three months. In it, Linda tells the story of one fishing trip and narrates the adventures she experienced on board with her five-man crew, including bad weather, sickness, mechanical problems and, of course, the fish.

But the world of fish and fishing is a man's world and it's not easy to find a word to describe Linda Greenlaw. In her own words, she says: 'I am a woman. I am a fisherman. I am not a "fisherwoman", "fisherlady" or "fishergirl".'

A man's world?

1 Replace the words in bold with a synonym.

1 Our school puts a lot of **importance** on passing exams. emphasis
2 I'm **responsible** for Human Resources in my company. ______
3 Firefighters took all night to **extinguish** the fire. ______
4 My sister is good at a lot of sports and she **does really well** at swimming. ______
5 My working hours are **changeable**. I don't start at the same time every day. ______
6 My grandmother is **slowly** recovering from her operation. ______
7 I'm very happy for my colleague. She has just got **a move to a better job**. ______
8 She should get the job because she has all the **necessary qualifications** and experience. ______
9 The game was **very difficult** because of the terrible weather conditions. ______
10 I don't **like** that man. I don't think he's honest. ______
11 Just before the car crashed, he put his hands over his head **without thinking**. ______
12 Marriage is supposed to be **an agreement** for life. ______
13 Police are questioning the **people that live there** about the recent burglaries. ______
14 You need to have many different **abilities** to work in an office. ______
15 I saw a documentary which **made me dislike** fur coats. ______

Professions

2 Solve the anagrams.

1 OTATNRASU A person who travels into space. ASTRONAUT
2 GUNRESO A person who performs operations. ______
3 OILSCOTIR A person who prepares legal documents. ______
4 TRAPERCNE A person who makes things from wood. ______
5 LBRUPEM A person who repairs water pipes. ______
6 LANECETCIRI A person who works with wires and cables. ______
7 DORITE A person who checks what an author writes. ______

Separable phrasal verbs

3 Complete the sentences with a word or expression from the box.

~~supply teacher~~ editor child psychologist barrister wholesaler financial analyst councillor

1 The downside to being a supply teacher is that you aren't at the school long enough to get to know your students very well.
2 As a ______, you have to use different techniques than when you're counselling an adult.
3 Only five years after starting his career in journalism, he was promoted to ______.
4 The drama of the courtroom was one aspect of being a ______ that had attracted her to the profession.
5 Shopkeepers buy their products from the ______ and then sell on to the customer at a higher price.
6 She was elected to serve the community as a town ______ last year.
7 More than one ______ has predicted that the recession will end this year.

4 Complete the sentences with the past simple of the phrasal verbs formed by joining a word in A to a word in B.

A	call give look make pick ~~take~~ tell turn
B	down off ~~off~~ off out up up up

1 I took off my coat as soon as I arrived.
2 She ______ ______ her son for making so much noise.
3 He hadn't done the homework, so he ______ ______ the answer.
4 Our teacher ______ ______ the exam results on the last day of term.
5 They ______ ______ the match because of rain.
6 My father ______ ______ my aunt from the station.
7 We ______ ______ the address on the internet.
8 He ______ ______ our invitation because he was busy.

5 Rewrite the sentences in exercise 4, using a pronoun.

1 I took it off as soon as I arrived.
2 She ______ for making so much noise.
3 He hadn't done the homework, so he ______.
4 Our teacher ______ on the last day of term.
5 They ______ because of rain.
6 My father ______ from the station.
7 We ______ on the internet.
8 He ______ because he was busy.

Defining relative clauses

1 Complete the sentences with the relative pronoun *who*, *which*, *where* or *whose*.

1 A rucksack is a bag which ________ you wear on your back.
2 Flip-flops are shoes ________ you wear on the beach.
3 A building site is a place ________ houses are built.
4 A widow is a woman ________ husband is dead.
5 A plumber is a person ________ repairs water pipes.
6 A surgery is ________ a doctor sees their patients.
7 A shoplifter is a person ________ steals from shops.
8 A successful writer is a person ________ books are published.

2 Rewrite the sentences with the relative pronoun *that* where possible.

1 A nanny is a person who looks after children.
A nanny is a person that looks after children.
2 A tag is a label which you attach to luggage.
____
3 A studio is where an artist works.
____
4 A surgeon is a doctor who performs operations.
____
5 A salary is the money which you earn in your job.
____
6 Leggings are trousers which girls wear.
____
7 An orphan is a person whose parents are dead.
____
8 An architect is a person who designs houses.
____

3 Rewrite the sentences that are incorrect.

1 A hospital is a place where ill people go there.
A hospital is a place where ill people go.
2 A musician is a person who he plays music.
____
3 A coat is a thing which you wear it in the winter.
____
4 He's the boy whose good at football.
____
5 A comedy is a film which makes you laugh.
____
6 That's the girl who her mother is a dentist.
____

4 Join the two sentences with a relative clause. Use the relative pronouns *who*, *which*, *where* or *whose*.

1 She's the receptionist. She answered my call.
She's the receptionist who answered my call.
2 That's the man. His dog scared me.
____
3 That's the sports shop. I bought my tracksuit there.
____
4 He's the shop assistant. He served me.
____
5 That's the jacket. I bought it in the sales.
____
6 A laboratory is a place. Scientists do experiments there.
____
7 That's the car. It was parked outside our house.
____
8 That's the woman. Her daughter is in my class.
____

CHALLENGE!

Continue the sentences.

1 A parent is a person who ________
2 Homework is something which ________
3 School is a place where ________
4 A teacher is a person whose ________

The world of work

1 Match the sentences with an adjective from the box.

challenging ~~menial~~ monotonous rewarding
skilled stressful

1 'I quite like my job, though the pay could be better. There's no scope for promotion but that suits me fine.' menial
2 'My job can be pretty demanding, especially at lunchtime when there are a lot of customers to serve.' _______
3 'I'm so lucky. I love my work. After so many years of study, I landed my ideal job.' _______
4 'I had relatively little experience when I started this job. The work has really stretched me at times, but I'm now in line for a promotion.' _______
5 'I don't mind my job. You sort of switch off, and I like the fact that I don't have to think too hard.' _______
6 'When I get a smile from one of the children, it's worth far more to me than a high salary.' _______

2 Find the eleven words in the word square that complete the activities below.

A	T	E	C	H	N	O	L	O	G	Y	L	M	D
M	B	D	X	E	F	G	H	I	Y	G	X	P	A
A	S	S	E	M	B	L	Y	L	I	N	E	D	T
C	T	R	A	A	F	H	X	B	N	W	O	R	A
H	U	C	S	L	D	M	E	P	K	P	Z	B	C
I	B	S	D	R	E	L	V	O	J	N	C	E	S
N	L	M	T	E	F	S	I	Q	T	F	K	U	G
E	Z	E	D	O	F	G	F	N	J	H	A	I	T
R	B	E	W	E	M	X	H	I	E	F	H	P	S
Y	C	T	E	A	M	E	P	N	G	S	R	B	O
A	B	I	Z	L	J	Z	R	B	S	U	E	L	M
C	O	N	T	R	A	C	T	S	J	V	R	W	P
A	M	G	O	V	X	K	O	T	W	U	X	E	D
Y	U	S	C	R	J	U	F	Z	I	D	E	A	S

1 deal with customers
2 draw up _______
3 report on _______ _______
4 work on an _______ _______
5 keep up with new _______
6 upload _______
7 operate _______
8 brainstorm _______
9 chair _______
10 liaise with a _______
11 meet _______

3 Match the jobs with the activities.

a call centre operator
b solicitor
c sales and marketing manager
d newspaper editor
e IT specialist
f factory worker

1 factory worker

operates machinery; works on an assembly line

2 _______

reports on sales figures; liaises with a team; brainstorms ideas

3 _______

chairs meetings; liaises with a team; meets deadlines; brainstorms ideas

4 _______

deals with customers

5 _______

draws up contracts

6 _______

uploads data; keeps up with new technology

CHALLENGE!

Write the name of one job you'd like to do, and say why. Write the name of one job you wouldn't like to do, and say why.

Non-defining relative clauses

1 Complete the sentences with a relative clause from the box.

who used to be Secretary General of the UN
where we usually go on holiday
which can be read at a distance
whose books include *The Kite Runner*
which is on the fourth floor
~~who was a German composer~~

1 Ludwig van Beethoven, who was a German composer, became deaf in later life.
2 My flat, ________________, is in the middle of town.
3 RFID tags, ________________, will be used by all supermarkets in the future.
4 Kofi Annan, ________________, had a twin sister.
5 Khaled Hosseini, ________________, was born in Afghanistan.
6 The island of Menorca, ________________, is in the Mediterranean.

2 Choose the correct relative pronoun.

1 Nelson Mandela, (**who**) / **that** was released from prison in 1990, became the first black South African president.
2 Berlin, **that** / **which** used to be divided into two parts, is now the capital of Germany.
3 Robert Louis Stevenson, **whose** / **who** books include *Treasure Island,* died in 1894.
4 Chernobyl, **where** / **whose** there was a nuclear disaster in 1986, is in the Ukraine.
5 Wolfgang Amadeus Mozart, **whose** / **who** wrote the famous opera *The Magic Flute*, first performed in public at the age of six.
6 Rigoberta Menchú, **that** / **who** won the Nobel Peace Prize in 1992, comes from Guatemala.

Nelson Mandela

Rigoberta Menchú

3 Rewrite the sentences that are incorrect.

1 Tenerife, where is a popular holiday destination, is in the Canary Islands.
Tenerife, which is a popular holiday destination
2 Jane Austen, who best known novel is *Sense and Sensibility*, had seven brothers and sisters.
3 Stockholm, that I went last year, is the capital of Sweden.
4 Ingrid Betancourt, whose kidnapping lasted six and a half years, is a Columbian-French politician.
5 My car, that I bought last year, is a cool yellow Mini.
6 Picasso, who paintings include *Guernica*, was born in Malaga, in the south of Spain.

4 Join the two sentences, adding the second sentence as a relative clause.

1 Crete has a lot of ancient history. It's the largest of the Greek islands.
Crete, which is the largest of the Greek Islands, has a lot of ancient history.
2 Julius Caesar was Emperor of Rome until 44 BC. He was killed by a former friend.
____
3 Mozart is one of the most popular classical composers. He died in poverty.
____
4 Dakar is the capital of Senegal. The famous car race ends there.
____
5 William Shakespeare was born in Stratford-upon-Avon. His plays include *Hamlet* and *Romeo and Juliet*.
____

CHALLENGE!

Write a sentence about your favourite writer or composer.

Charles Dickens, who is one of the greatest English novelists, was born in 1812.

A job application

Preparation

1 Put the words in the correct order.

1 gardener / the post / for / I am writing / of / to apply
I am writing to apply for the post of gardener.

2 CV / enclosing / I / am / my
______

3 person / discuss / in / We / my / could / application
______

4 responsibilities / planting / there / as well as / My / included / garden design
______

5 gardening / in / have / I / experience / considerable
______

6 be / work / on 15th May / available / I / to start / will
______

7 a reference / can / necessary / I / if / supply
______

2 Complete the letter with the expressions from exercise 1.

Dear Sir or Madam

[1] *I am writing to apply for the post of gardener* for the City Council, which was advertised in last Sunday's newspaper. [2] ______. For the last two years I have worked for a private gardening company in Bristol. [3] ______.

I consider myself to be a reliable and enthusiastic worker. [4] ______ from the manager of the company where I am working at present.

I would be very grateful for the opportunity to visit your department, so that [5] ______. I am available for interview any afternoon after 3 p.m.

If my application is successful, [6] ______ when I am planning to leave my present company.

[7] ______

Yours faithfully

Nick Baxter

3 Number the questions in the order they are answered in Nick's letter.

A What are your responsibilities? ☐
B What personal qualities make you suitable? ☐
C Are you sending in a CV? ☐
D When are you available for an interview? ☐
E When are you available to start work? ☐
F Which post are you applying for? 1
G How did you find out about the job? ☐
H Where are you working now? ☐
I Can you provide a reference? ☐

Writing task

4 In your notebook write a letter of application for the posts advertised below. Use the Writing Bank on page 91 to help you. Write 150–200 words and do the following:

- make notes on the answers to the questions in exercise 3
- organize your notes into paragraphs.

Sports monitors

Wanted for council summer camps.
Excellent opportunity to gain experience working with children aged 6–14 in beautiful surroundings.
Must be fit and enjoy playing sport.

£1,000 a month

Check your work

Have you

☐ started and finished your letter appropriately?
☐ organized your letter into paragraphs?
☐ written 150–200 words?
☐ checked grammar, spelling and punctuation?

SELF CHECK 3: GRAMMAR

1 Complete the questions, using the relative pronouns *who*, *which*, *where* and *whose*.

1 Did you see the man who_____ was driving that car?
2 Did you post the letter _________ I gave you this morning?
3 Do you remember the name of the hospital _________ you were born?
4 Do you know the teacher _________ class won the competition?
5 Have the police searched the house _________ the crime occurred?
6 Did you talk to the girl _________ father is a lawyer?
7 Did the boy _________ broke his leg go to hospital?
8 Have you tidied up the books _________ fell on the floor?

Your score ___ **/8**

2 Match the sentence halves and join them with the relative pronouns *who*, *which*, *where* or *whose*.

1 Mount Everest is in Nepal.
2 Yuri Gagarin died in a flying accident in 1968.
3 Kuala Lumpur is the capital city of Malaysia.
4 Michael Phelps won eight gold medals at the 2008 Olympic Games.
5 The painter Van Gogh cut off his own ear.
6 Sabeer Bhatia is originally from India.
7 The River Nile flows into the Mediterranean Sea.
8 Machu Picchu is a major tourist attraction in Peru.

A His works include *Sunflowers*.
B He founded the company Hotmail in 1996.
C His favourite sport is swimming.
D It is the longest river in the world.
E He was the first man in space.
F You can see the Petronas Towers there.
G The Incas once lived there.
H It is the highest mountain in the world.

1 Mount Everest, which is the highest mountain in the world, is in Nepal.
2 _________________________
3 _________________________
4 _________________________
5 _________________________
6 _________________________
7 _________________________
8 _________________________

Your score ___ **/16**

3 Choose the correct relative pronoun.

1 Sydney, **who** / **which** / **where** / **whose** the 2000 Olympic Games took place, is famous for its opera house.
2 Tim Berners-Lee, **who** / **which** / **where** / **whose** parents were both mathematicians, is the founder of the World Wide Web.
3 Neil Armstrong, **who** / **which** / **where** / **whose** was the first man to land on the moon, is now retired.
4 The Taj Mahal, **who** / **which** / **where** / **whose** was built in the seventeenth century, is in Agra in India.
5 Guglielmo Marconi, **who** / **which** / **where** / **whose** invented the radio, was an Italian physicist.
6 The Egyptian Museum, **who** / **which** / **where** / **whose** you can see King Tutankhamun's treasures, is located in Cairo.
7 Charles Dickens, **who** / **which** / **where** / **whose** novels include *David Copperfield*, is a nineteenth-century English novelist.
8 The island of Madagascar, **who** / **which** / **where** / **whose** is off the southeast coast of Africa, has many unique animals and plants.

Your score ___ **/8**

4 Write relative clauses about the words in the box.

a library a match a mechanic a neighbour an orphan ~~a paper clip~~ a skilled worker a zebra crossing

1 It holds paper together.
A paper clip is a thing which holds paper together.
2 He has special qualifications.
____
3 You can cross the road there.
____
4 Her house is next to yours.
____
5 He repairs cars.
____
6 It makes fire.
____
7 You can borrow books here.
____
8 His parents have died.
____

Your score ___ **/8**

Total ___ **/40**

SELF CHECK 3: VOCABULARY

1 Complete the vocabulary quiz with words from Unit 3.

Quiz

1 He worked in local government as a ____________ servant until his retirement.

2 It's cheaper to buy goods direct from a ____________.

3 When the stone came towards him, he ____________ protected his face.

4 A flight ____________ serves drinks on a plane.

5 When chairing ____________, it is necessary to give everyone a chance to air their views.

6 We picked ____________ my brother from the airport.

7 She's in ____________ of interviewing job applicants.

8 Stephen is hoping to get a ____________ to Head of Department.

9 The job ____________ include three years' experience and a working knowledge of computers.

10 The most ____________ job I ever had was in a restaurant kitchen. It was both physically hard and mentally demanding.

11 My working hours are very ____________, so I can start and finish when I want.

12 She was embarrassed when her employer eventually discovered that she had made ____________ the qualifications and experience on her CV.

13 His job as a ____________ meant that he spent long hours away from home on the road.

14 I used to want to be a hairdresser, but I was put ____________ by having to stand all day.

15 A ____________ teacher teaches very little children.

16 It is essential to observe health and safety guidelines if your job involves operating ____________.

17 A coal ____________ has one of the dirtiest jobs.

18 My mother ____________ me off for arriving late.

19 The job requires computer ____________.

20 They called ____________ the barbecue because of the rain.

Your score /20

2 Complete the text with the correct form of the words in brackets.

A dream come true

Jon Bennett used to run a hotel, which he found quite [1] ____________ (stress) but now he has a very different job. The [2] ____________ (require) of his new job are quite unusual, but Jon says he gets a lot out of it and finds it very [3] ____________ (reward). Every day Jon has to climb Helvellyn, a mountain in the Lake District, to check the weather conditions at the summit. The [4] ____________ (inform) which he gathers is then passed to the Lake District telephone Weatherline service. The Weatherline is used by nearly half a million walkers every year. Although Helvellyn is only 950 metres tall, weather conditions at the summit can change rapidly and make the ascent too [5] ____________ (challenge) for even the most [6] ____________ (skill) climbers.

When Jon was a child, he lived in Buckinghamshire, in the south of England, but he often visited the Lake District on family holidays and he [7] ____________ (gradual) fell in love with it. He studied catering at college and took the first opportunity to move north and find a job in a hotel in the area. When he saw the [8] ____________ (advertise) for the job with Weatherline, he jumped at the opportunity, and sent in his [9] ____________ (apply) immediately. He couldn't believe his luck when they told him he'd got the job.

Even though Jon has no chance of [10] ____________ (promote), he still loves his job. 'It's a dream come true!' he says.

Your score /10

Total /30

4 Body and mind

READING

Before reading: Fast food

1 Which of the foods in the box below contain the most

1 fat? butter
2 sugar? ______
3 vitamins? ______
4 carbohydrates? ______
5 protein? ______
6 salt? ______

~~butter~~ carrots crisps eggs pasta sweets

2 Complete the summary of the text about obesity. Use the words in the box.

bill dismissed lawsuits sue

In 2002, a group of obese teenagers tried to [1] ______ McDonald's for making them fat. The judge supported McDonald's and [2] ______ the case. Subsequent [3] ______ against fast food companies have also failed and on top of that, the US government has passed a [4] ______ protecting the food industry.

3 Read the text about the film *Super Size Me*. What effect did Morgan Spurlock's experiment have on his health?

Super Size Me

Super Size Me is a 2004 film by Morgan Spurlock in which he documents his experiment to eat only McDonald's fast food three times a day, every day, for thirty days.

Spurlock made himself a short list of rules for the experiment, including an obligation to eat all of the three meals he ordered. He also had to 'Super Size', which means accepting a giant portion every time the option was offered to him. He ended up vomiting after the first Super Size meal he finished, after taking nearly twenty minutes to consume it.

After five days, Spurlock put on almost 5kg, and he soon found himself feeling depressed, with no energy. The only thing that got rid of his headaches and made him feel better was another McDonald's meal, so his doctors told him he was addicted. More seriously, around day twenty, he started experiencing heart palpitations and one of the doctors detected liver problems. However, in spite of his doctor's advice, Spurlock continued to the end of the month and achieved a total weight gain of 11kg. His body mass index also increased from a healthy 23.2 to an overweight 27.

It took Spurlock fifteen months to recover from his experiment and return to his original weight, but the film also had a wider impact. Just after its showing in 2004, McDonald's phased out the Super Size option and healthier options like salads appeared on the menu. Unfortunately, McDonald's deny the connection between the film and the changes, but it is interesting to note how closely they coincided with the release of the film.

4 Are the sentences true or false? Write T or F.

1 Morgan Spurlock carried out the experiment on himself. ___
2 He had to eat a Super Size meal once a week. ___
3 Nothing could get rid of Spurlock's headaches. ___
4 The experiment affected Spurlock's heart and liver. ___
5 Spurlock stopped the experiment early because of his doctor's warnings. ___
6 Afterwards, it took Spurlock five months to return to his original weight. ___
7 As a result of the film, McDonald's has changed its menus. ___

CHALLENGE!

Decribe your favourite healthy meal.

The memory man

1 Complete the sentences with a word in the box.

achievement ~~apply~~ associate benefit catapulted dull essentially inspired knowledge manoeuvre memorized pantry stumbled sundial visualize

1 I've seen an advert for an accountant in the newspaper and I'm going to apply for the job.
2 Do you know how to tell the time on a ________?
3 He made a mistake because he'd ________ the formula wrongly.
4 The player was ________ to fame when he beat the current champion in the final.
5 Their greatest ________ was winning the World Cup.
6 A paramedic is ________ a doctor, but with fewer qualifications.
7 Who is going to ________ from the new tax cuts?
8 The teacher asked us to ________ our perfect home and write about it.
9 His trip to Thailand ________ him to look for a job in a travel agency.
10 My car is very big and I find it very difficult to ________.
11 I'm tired of my ________ existence, so I'm planning a world trip with a friend.
12 I'm surprised it's so cold – I don't usually ________ Spain with snow and ice!
13 She has a very wide ________ of history.
14 There's a ________ in our kitchen, where we keep food that doesn't need to go in the fridge.
15 He ________ over a rock in the path and only just managed to stop himself from falling.

Word formation: verbs

2 Complete the sentences with the correct verb form of the word in brackets.

1 My brother's attitude exemplifies the way boys think in my country nowadays. (example)
2 We tried to ________ the document so that everybody would understand it. (simple)
3 I recognize the name, but I can't ________ her face. (visual)
4 Last year the govenment's immigration policy ________ a lot of its supporters. (alien)
5 The council has decided to ________ an emergency plan because of the bad weather. (active)
6 They ________ the event in the press, so everybody knew about it. (public)
7 We asked the head teacher to ________ the rules on school uniform. (clear)
8 The teachers find it very difficult to ________ between the twins in my class. (different)

Compound adjectives

3 Complete the compound adjectives with the words in the box.

blooded haired handed ~~kind~~ level minded short thick

1 kind - hearted
2 narrow - ________
3 ________ - headed
4 fair - ________
5 ________ - skinned
6 cold - ________
7 ________ - sighted
8 right - ________

4 Rewrite the sentences, using a compound adjective from exercise 3.

1 You don't use your left hand for doing things.
You're ________.
2 I can only see things that are very close to me.
I'm ________.
3 The murderer expressed no guilt about his crimes.
He was quite ________.
4 Our class tutor never seems to take offence.
He's quite ________.
5 His brothers and sisters have dark hair, but he's blond.
He's ________.
6 My father never panics.
He's very ________.
7 Sara thinks she's always right. She never listens to what anybody else says.
She's really ________.
8 My aunt spends most of her time helping other people.
She's very ________.

Past simple and present perfect contrast

1 **Complete the postcard. Choose the correct alternatives.**

Dear All,
We're here in Monaco to see the Grand Prix. We [1] **arrived / have arrived** last Tuesday and we [2] **were / have been** here for four days now. So far we [3] **saw / have seen** the palace and we [4] **visited / have visited** a museum. Yesterday we [5] **had / have had** a tour of Monte Carlo and in the evening we [6] **went / have been** to a nice restaurant, where we [7] **ate / have eaten** good food. At breakfast the tour guide [8] **gave / has given** us our tickets for the race. We're really excited!
Jack, Betty, Rob and Nick

2 **Complete the sentences. Use the past simple in one sentence and the present perfect in the other.**

1 **go**
I *'ve been* to a Formula One race three times.
Tom's tired because he ______ to a concert last night.

2 **lose**
Mike ______ his wallet, so he didn't have any money.
Kim's upset because she ______ her mobile phone.

3 **have**
I ______ a pet cat when I was little.
Brad's dog is very old. He ______ Rex for thirteen years.

4 **break**
Linda's in hospital because she ______ her arm.
Lionel ______ his leg while he was playing rugby.

3 **Match the sentences using the present perfect in exercise 2 with the uses below.**

We use the present perfect
a to say how long a current situation has existed. ____
b to talk about an experience in the past. ____
c to talk about events that are connected with the present. ____ ____

4 **Complete the text with the verbs in the box in the past simple or the present perfect.**

go not miss score see ~~take~~

When I was eight, my dad [1] *took* me to see my first football match. It was Manchester United v Arsenal, and since that day, I [2] ______ one single match. On one occasion I even [3] ______ when I had a serious case of flu! So far I [4] ______ my team score over a hundred goals, but the best goal ever was the one David Beckham [5] ______ against Wimbledon in August 1996.

5 **Complete the information about world champion racing driver, Fernando Alonso. Use the past simple or the present perfect form of the verbs in brackets.**

Fernando Alonso [1] *was born* (be born) in Oviedo, northern Spain, in 1981. When he was three his father [2] ______ (build) him a go-kart and as a child he [3] ______ (travel) around Spain participating in karting competitions. In 1996 he [4] ______ (win) the Junior World Cup.
He [5] ______ (start) racing cars when he was eighteen and drove in his first Formula One race in 2001. In 2003 he [6] ______ (become) the youngest driver ever to win a Formula One race, when he [7] ______ (come) first in the Hungarian Grand Prix.
Since then he [8] ______ (be) the Formula One world champion twice. He [9] ______ (just change) back from the McLaren team to the Renault team, so his colours will be changing back again, too.
Fernando doesn't live in Spain any more, as he [10] ______ (move) to Oxford in England. He [11] ______ (buy) a house near Lake Geneva, too. In February 2006 he [12] ______ (ask) the singer Raquel del Rosario to marry him.

CHALLENGE!

Write two or more sentences about an important event you have seen. Use the past simple and the present perfect.

Body idioms

1 **Complete the parts of the body. Add *a*, *e*, *i*, *o* and *u*. Then match the words with the pictures (A–T).**

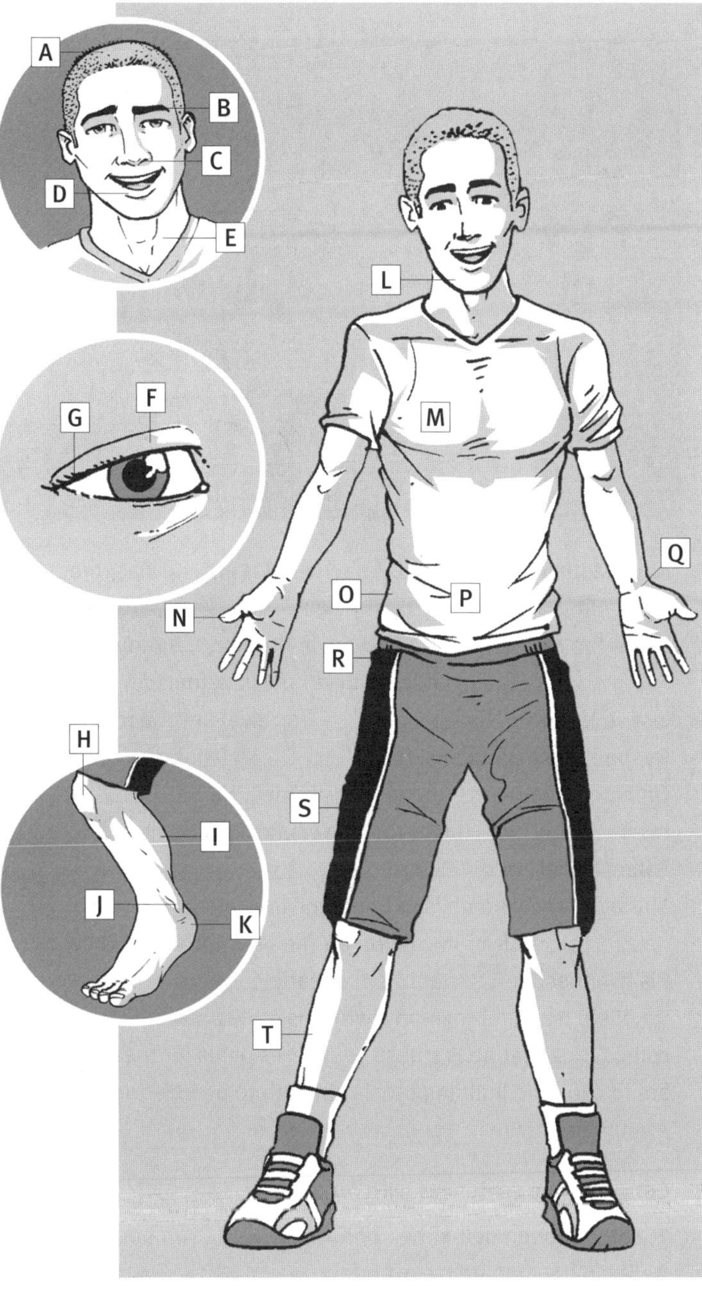

1 th_u_mb	N	11 st__m__ch	______
2 th__gh	______	12 __y__br__w	______
3 sh__n	______	13 thr__ __t	______
4 h__ __l	______	14 h__p	______
5 l__p	______	15 __nkl__	______
6 sc__lp	______	16 w__ __st	______
7 n__str__l	______	17 __y__l__d	______
8 __y__l__sh	______	18 ch__n	______
9 c__lf	______	19 wr__st	______
10 ch__st	______	20 kn__ __	______

2 **Match the words in the box with the definitions (1–8). There are two words that you do not need.**

blood ~~brain~~ heart liver lungs muscles ribs spine skin stomach

1 The _brain_ controls your thoughts, feelings and movements.
2 The ______ sends blood around your body.
3 The ______ is your backbone.
4 The ______ are used for breathing.
5 ______ is a red liquid that travels though your body.
6 The ______ cleans your blood.
7 The ______ are bones which go round your chest and protect the organs.
8 The ______ is where food goes after you've eaten it.

3 **Complete the body idioms with the correct part of the body.**

1 OK, I'm sorry. There's no need to bite my _head_ off.
2 I really put my ______ in it when I asked her about her party. I didn't know it was a surprise!
3 Don't worry, she isn't being serious. She's only pulling your ______.
4 Could you keep an ______ on my bag while I get a coffee?
5 He keeps interfering in things that are none of his business. I wish he'd stop poking his ______ into my affairs.
6 Whether she went to Jane's or Frank's party is splitting ______. The fact is that she lied about staying in to do her homework.
7 They were really keen at first but I think they're getting cold ______.
8 It's better to get something off your ______ than to keep worrying about it in private.
9 He said he didn't want to contribute to our campaign, but I'm hoping that I can twist his ______.
10 Nobody seems to know what's happening about the plans for tonight, so I think we'll have to play it by ______.

CHALLENGE!

Describe your most recent aches and pains.

Present perfect continuous

1 Complete the sentences with the present perfect continuous of the verbs in brackets.

1 Michael has been playing handball for ten years. (play)
2 His neighbours ________ since he cut down the tree. (complain)
3 Tom ________ mountains since he was a child. (climb)
4 She's got a sore throat because she ________ all evening. (shout)
5 Johnny and Roger ________ for very long. (not painting)
6 They're not very good because they ________. (not practise)
7 Tania ________ her own accounts for the last year. (do)
8 She's fed up because they ________ to her advice. (not listen)

2 Match each sentence in exercise 1 with the uses of the present perfect continuous below.

a An action that began in the past and is still in progress. 1 ___ ___ ___ ___ ___
b An action that has recently stopped and that explains the present situation. ___ ___ ___

3 Choose the present perfect simple or present perfect continuous.

1 She can't play hockey today because **she's broken** / **she's been breaking** her arm.
2 **She's liked** / **She's been liking** pizza since she went to Italy.
3 Adrian **has flown** / **has been flying** to New York since he became a pilot.
4 They can't go on holiday because **they've crashed** / **they've been crashing** their car.
5 So far **they've played** / **they've been playing** in twelve different countries.
6 Our science teacher **has only been teaching** / **has only taught** in two other schools
7 **We've seen** / **We've been seeing** the Harlem Globetrotters five times.
8 **I've been reading** / **I've read** the biography of Lewis Hamilton, but I'm only on page 57.

4 Complete the text about the tennis player Andy Murray with the present perfect simple or the present perfect continuous of the verbs in brackets.

Andy Murray [1] ________ (play) tennis since he was three years old. Since April 2007, the Scot [2] ________ (be) one of the top ten male tennis players in the world. Although he [3] ________ (train) with the best fitness trainers for the last seven years, he [4] ________ (receive) several injuries. Despite these problems, he [5] ________ (win) matches in Qatar, at Wimbledon and in the US Open. He [6] ________ even ________ (beat) top players Roger Federer and Rafael Nadal.
Murray's family home is in Dunblane in Scotland, but he [7] ________ (live) in London for the past few years. Only in his twenties, he [8] ________ already ________ (publish) his autobiography, which is quite an achievement considering that he is still so young. His plans for the future are to continue building up his strength to be able to win even more titles.

5 Complete the sentences with *for* or *since*.

1 They've been doing their homework ______ an hour.
2 She's been doing taekwondo ______ 1990.
3 He's been playing for England ______ ten years.
4 I've been studying German ______ six months.
5 We've been skiing ______ we were children.
6 I've been sneezing ______ yesterday.

CHALLENGE!

Write about your favourite sportsperson.

____
____
____

An informal letter: giving news

Preparation

1 **Read the letter and answer the questions.**

1 Why hasn't Susan written before?
2 Where does she want to go?
3 What is Susan's news about her sister?

Dear Clara,

Sorry I haven't written for ages, but I've had a good excuse. I was rollerblading down a hill with a wall at the bottom and I broke both my wrists when I tried to stop myself. Stupid, or what?

Enough of all that. What about you? What have you been up to? If you've been studying as hard as me, you're probably completely fed up. Why don't we plan a trip for the end of the exams? I quite fancy going to Venice for a weekend. What do you think?

Guess what? My sister's got a new job in France. She's moving to Paris next month. I'll really miss her, but she's very excited about it. She sends her love.

I'd better stop now as it's getting late. Do write and tell me what you think about my idea.

Lots of love,

Susan

2 **Match the highlighted phrases in the letter with the functions below.**

1 making a suggestion
Why don't we
2 making a strong request
______
3 sending greetings from someone else
______
4 changing the subject
______
5 ending the letter
______
6 introducing surprising news
______
7 asking for news of the other person
______

3 **Complete the phrases for beginning a letter with a suitable word.**

1 Sorry I haven't ______ for ages.
2 It was great to ______ from you.
3 Thanks ______ your letter.
4 How ______ you?

4 **Complete the phrases for ending a letter with the expressions in the box.**

better go now. getting late. me for dinner.
news for now. out of space.

1 That's all my ______
2 Must dash – Mum's calling ______
3 I'd better finish here as I'm running ______
4 I'd better stop here. It's ______
5 That's all for now. I'd ______

Writing task

5 **In your notebook write a letter to a friend who is studying abroad. Use the Writing Bank on page 90 to help you. Write 150–200 words and include this information:**

- some news about yourself
- a suggestion for meeting up somewhere soon
- some news about your friends or family.

Check your work

Have you

☐ started and finished your letter appropriately?
☐ organized your letter into paragraphs?
☐ used some functional phrases?
☐ written 150–200 words?
☐ checked grammar, spelling and punctuation?

SELF CHECK 4: GRAMMAR

1 Complete the sentences with the past simple or the present perfect form of the verb in brackets.

1 I ________ my best friend since I was 8. (know)
2 We ________ on holiday last year. (not go)
3 The children ________ yet. (not get up)
4 My brother ________ for ten jobs so far. (apply)
5 I feel awful because I ________ my mother's birthday yesterday. (forget)
6 Lara ________ her arm a year ago and it still hurts. (break)
7 William is exhausted. He ________ for a week. (not sleep)
8 My teacher couldn't use her car this morning because it ________ any petrol. (not have)
9 They ________ opposite us for ten years before moving to the United States. (live)
10 We ________ our cousins in Australia for ages. (not see)
11 Mr Winter ________ at this school since 1985. (be)

Your score ____ **/11**

2 Use the past simple or the present perfect to write questions with the words.

1 What time / you / go to bed / last night?
____
2 How many exams / Jamie / take / so far?
____
3 you / spoke / to your cousins / since / their visit?
____
4 your family / live / in the same house / ten years ago?
____
5 Colin / tidy / his room / yet?
____
6 When / Gloria / meet / her best friend?
____
7 Where / you / be / yesterday morning?
____
8 your brother / finish / his homework / already?
____
9 he / see / the new Bond film / yet ?
____
10 What / you / have / for dinner / last night ?
____
11 anyone / come / to collect the parcel / earlier ?
____

Your score ____ **/11**

3 Complete the sentences with the same verb. Use the present perfect simple in one sentence and the present perfect continuous in the other.

1 clean
a My aunt ________ her car. It looks much better now.
b My mother ________ the house all morning. She hasn't done the living room yet.

2 read
a I ________ the book you lent me. I'm about half way through.
b I ________ *A Thousand Splendid Suns*. It was really good.

3 cut
a She isn't really crying; she ________ the onions for dinner.
b She ________ her finger, and it really hurts.

4 run
a He's hot because he ________.
b He ________ several marathons in his life, but he doesn't train any more.

5 do
a We aren't at home because we ________ the shopping.
b The fridge is full because we ________ the shopping.

Your score ____ **/10**

4 Complete the text with the past perfect simple or continuous form of the verbs in the box.

be book look look forward to plan study suggest visit

I [1] ________ French for eight years now and so has my brother. We like travelling to France and we [2] ________ there lots of times together. We [3] ________ Bordeaux, Toulouse and Marseilles, but we've never been to Paris. We're going there next month. We [4] ________ a hotel right in the city centre and we [5] ________ on the internet to find the best places to visit. So far we [6] ________ to visit the Louvre and the Eiffel Tower. A friend of ours [7] ________ going on a boat trip on the River Seine, which also sounds nice. We [8] ________ to our trip for a long time, so I hope we won't be disappointed.

Your score ____ **/8**

Total ____ **/40**

SELF CHECK 4: VOCABULARY

1 Complete the vocabulary quiz with words from Unit 4.

Quiz

1 My greatest __________ was passing my finals when I was at university.
2 We weren't sure of the rules, so we asked the teacher to __________ them.
3 Alan twisted his _____ _____ while he was playing football.
4 When you need to watch someone's belongings, you keep an __________ on them.
5 Your general __________ is really good – why don't you go on a quiz show on TV?
6 They don't want anyone to know about their successful deal, so they aren't going to __________ it.
7 Your __________ connect your back and your legs.
8 He's so __________ that he sometimes wears glasses over his contact lenses.
9 I don't __________ your brother with sport. When did he start playing handball?
10 When they saw the man coming towards them, they decided to __________ the alarm.
11 Your __________ connects your hand to your arm.
12 The only way to learn the grammar rules of Latin is to __________ them.
13 Are you going to __________ for a new job?
14 My grandfather never listens to the opinions of other people. He's very __________.
15 She called a friend to get the problem off her __________.
16 Someone who is colour-blind can usually see colours but finds it hard to _____ _____ between them.
17 Everyone will __________ from the cut in the price of petrol.
18 I'm usually quite __________, but my sister's comment really upset me.
19 You really put your __________ in it when you asked her about her exam results.
20 My grandma was a very modern woman and she __________ my mum to follow a rewarding career.

Your score /20

2 Complete the text with the correct words (a–d).

When I saw the maths expert Alberto Coto in action, I was surprised [1] __________ how normal he looked. I have always [2] __________ extreme intelligence with mad scientists, so at first I hardly noticed the slightly [3] __________ young man on the stage.

I hadn't really wanted to attend the show, but a friend had twisted my [4] __________. She told me Mr Coto could guess somebody's birthday by doing a few sums, but I thought she must be pulling my [5] __________. However, during that evening I witnessed this and several other tricks where Mr Coto had to [6] __________ long lists of numbers.

Alberto Coto is no mad scientist. He is a [7] __________ maths expert with a desire to help others improve their minds. He is the current world champion in mental arithmetic but his [8] __________ have not been widely [9] __________. He spends his time travelling around schools and universities, motivating students in the field of mathematics.

If you get the chance to see Alberto Coto demonstrate his [10] __________, you really must go. The man is truly a genius.

	a	b	c	d
1	on	at	in	with
2	recognized	joined	associated	known
3	short-visioned	short-seeing	short-eyed	short-sighted
4	arm	leg	hand	foot
5	hair	finger	leg	nose
6	memorize	concentrate	think	remind
7	level-minded	level-headed	big-headed	narrow-minded
8	achievements	successions	goals	managements
9	advertised	communicated	publicized	told
10	knows	knowledge	knowing	knew

Your score /10

Total /30

5 Our future

READING

Before reading: Visions of the future

1 Match the sentence beginnings (1–7) with the endings (a–g).

1 The hole in the ozone layer will get bigger if factories do not reduce d
2 The advances in medical research mean that now we can treat ___
3 If we do not prevent global warming, the earth will suffer ___
4 In the next fifty years, some countries will have started ___
5 With genetic engineering, doctors will soon be able to replace ___
6 Computers will soon be providing ___
7 By the end of the century, scientists may have made ___

a us with more than just factual information.
b important discoveries about immortality.
c a terrible catastrophe.
d their carbon emissions.
e old and injured parts of the body.
f illnesses more effectively.
g a colony in space.

2 Read the text about the film *WALL-E*. What mesages about the future of Earth and the human race is the film trying to convey?

3 Complete the text with the missing sentences. There is one extra sentence you do not need to use.

A On the Axiom, man has become completely dependent on robots.
B WALL-E and the robot arrive on the spaceship with the plant.
C WALL-E has stayed behind to clear up the mess.
D WALL-E shows his emotions with hand gestures, facial expressions and robotic sounds.
E The simple act of getting out of a chair and standing up is considered an achievement.
F The robot's job is to look for and analyze any sign of life it encounters on the planet.

WALL-E – A VISION OF THE FUTURE?

WALL-E is Pixar's ninth full-length feature film and the second directed by Andrew Stanton, whose first movie was the delightful *Finding Nemo*. *WALL-E* tells the story of a lonely robot's search for friendship in a world which is covered in rubbish. About 700 years from now, pollution produced by the Buy-N-Large Corporation has forced humans to leave planet Earth. 1____ And he doesn't mind his job stacking rubbish into tidy cubes which go on to form the bricks of giant buildings made of rubbish. It also gives him the opportunity to collect some of the stranger objects he finds, like a Rubik's cube, a tennis ball and an old video. However, *WALL-E*'s existence is very quiet and lonely and his only friend is a cockroach.

WALL-E's life suddenly changes when an enormous spaceship drops a second robot on the Earth. 2____ When the robot finds a small green plant in an unexpected place, it is required to return to the spaceship Axiom to deliver it. *WALL-E* decides to accompany the robot.

It is during the second half of the film that we see what has become of human beings since they left the Earth. 3____ This has turned them into big, fat, lazy beings who spend all their lives sitting in front of computer screens. Their legs have got shorter and are no longer able to support the weight of the huge bodies they were made to carry. 4____ Communication between the humans takes place with the person on the screen in front of them; they fail to even notice those in front or behind, to their right or left on their aimless ride around the spaceship. 5____ In the right hands this small green shoot could bring environmental balance back to the planet that man has destroyed.

The story is engaging, the main character is extremely lovable and the music is superb. One of Pixar's best films, *WALL-E* will probably go on to be considered one of the greatest animated movies ever created.

Fifty years on

1 Replace the words in bold with a synonym.

1 The doctors **made** her **well again** with antibiotics and total bed rest. treated
2 The company **gives** the volunteers food and accommodation while they are abroad. ______
3 My uncle is suffering from a disease that the doctors say is **possibly going to kill him.** ______
4 All of my brothers and sisters are quite **intelligent.** ______
5 Many countries are trying to **make** their carbon emissions **smaller.** ______
6 When the shop started its sale, everybody **went in large numbers** to find a bargain. ______
7 The main problem of the prison system is **there are too many people.** ______
8 People who lose a leg do not expect it to **grow again.** ______
9 I always use the same **programme that looks for information.** ______
10 My father wants to **start** his own company. ______
11 The plane avoided a **disaster** by performing an emergency landing in the river. ______
12 The robot was **not working properly** and it kept on crashing into the wall. ______
13 Many children in the world have lost **arms and legs** because of landmines. ______
14 They tried to **talk in a logical way** with their son, but he couldn't see their point. ______
15 Annie is trilingual and so she easily found a job **translating spontaneously.** ______

Compound nouns

2 Join a word from box A to a word from box B to form compound nouns. Match the compound nouns to the definitions.

A ~~acid~~ endangered greenhouse ozone rain solar

B effect forest layer power ~~rain~~ species

1 Water containing dangerous chemicals that falls from the sky. acid rain
2 An area of jungle in tropical parts of the world. ______
3 Energy generated by the sun. ______
4 Animals and plants that may become extinct soon. ______
5 The process which makes the temperature of the Earth's atmosphere warmer. ______
6 Part of the atmoshere that helps protect the Earth from the sun's rays. ______

Verb + noun collocations

3 Complete the sentences with the compound nouns from exercise 2.

1 The greenhouse effect has been linked to global warming, which could cause the ice-caps to melt and sea levels to rise.
2 The ______ absorbs over 90% of the ultraviolet light we receive from the sun.
3 ______, like the orangutan, may not exist by the end of the century.
4 ______ works best in areas where there is a lot of sun.
5 ______ has destroyed many forests in central Europe.
6 The Amazon ______ contains over 30% of the animal and plant species on Earth.

4 Complete the sentences with the correct form of the verbs in the box.

achieve avoid do make prevent provide reduce ~~treat~~

1 Doctors are using revolutionary new medicines to treat the illness.
2 Most governments are trying to ______ climate change by passing a number of measures.
3 Countries which do not ______ the targets established by the Kyoto protocol should be fined.
4 Experts ______ an important discovery about wind energy recently.
5 Future leaders need to ______ the mistakes made in previous policies.
6 Scientists have spent several years ______ research into the effect of global warming.
7 The management refuses to ______ any information about the salaries of company directors.
8 Airlines are looking for an alternative fuel which will ______ their carbon emissions.

Modals and first conditional

1 **Complete the predictions with *will* (✓), *won't* (✗), *may* (?), or *might not* (?) and the verbs in brackets.**

What did our readers think about the future?

1 60% think books will disappear (✓) in the future. (disappear)
2 65% said libraries ______ (?) any more. (exist)
3 55% said employees ______ (?) from home. (work)
4 50% said commuters ______ (✗) by helicopter. (travel)
5 50% said cars ______ (?) on solar power. (run)
6 60% said robots ______ (?) our food. (cook)
7 70% said people ______ (✗) more than one child. (have)
8 75% said CDs ______ (✓) obsolete. (become)

2 **Use the pictures to write first conditional sentences.**

1

If John passes his driving test, he'll buy a new car.
(pass driving test, buy car)

2

If he ______, he'll ______.
(go to university, study medicine)

3

If he ______, ______.
(get married, have two children)

4

If ______, ______.
(have enough money, travel to Australia)

5

If ______, ______.
(can find a job, work as a doctor)

3 **Match the two halves of the sentences.**

1 If the rainforests are cut down, d
2 If we don't invest in renewable energies, ___
3 If we don't save water, ___
4 If we don't recycle our rubbish, ___
5 If the polar ice caps melt, ___
6 If we don't protect endangered species, ___
7 If we don't control factory waste, ___
8 If we encourage countries to disarm, ___

a many rivers will be poisoned.
b we won't be able to use electricity in our houses.
c there might not be a nuclear war.
d we won't have enough oxygen.
e they might become extinct.
f many people may drown.
g there may be a terrible drought.
h the world will turn into one big dustbin.

CHALLENGE!

How do you see your future? Write a sentence about

your studies: ______

your job: ______

your family: ______

your home: ______

Gadgets

1 Re-order the letters and complete the puzzle.

1 vancontenoilun
2 vatininove
3 yakwc
4 testa fo het tra
5 rolabu-snivag
6 comebitri
7 lagditi
8 coe-lidyfren
9 sicon
10 meltutia
11 ledsrosc

2 Match the definitions (1–11) with the expressions from the puzzle in exercise 1.

1 connected to sound waves sonic
2 funny or unusual ______
3 storing or recording information electronically ______
4 not harming the environment ______
5 new and original ______
6 not connected to power sources with cables or wires ______
7 saving you time and effort ______
8 ultra-modern ______
9 the best example of something ______
10 using human features for identification ______
11 non-standard ______

3 Choose the correct option.

Not long ago, the idea of carrying out surveillance on your pet was [1] **innovative / unconventional**, or even a bit [2] **digital / wacky**. Not any more. This [3] **sonic / innovative** gadget is the [4] **cordless / ultimate** present for you and your pet. As soon as your pet enters a specific room or area inside your house, it triggers a [5] **labour-saving / biometric** device that recognizes your pet and sends an alert to your mobile. You can choose to see a photo or video of your pet taken at that particular moment. With our [6] **unconventional / state-of-the-art** technology, you can keep an eye on your pet wherever you are in the world. And don't forget, this device is [7] **cordless / digital**, so there's no danger of your pet tripping over any cables.

CHALLENGE!

Think of a gadget or invention that is new, or invent one yourself. Say what it does and why you think it will catch on.

Future perfect and future continuous

1 Choose the correct alternatives to complete the speech by environmentalist David Greenan.

2 Read Anne's life plan and complete the sentences with the future continuous or the future perfect.

1 By 2015 Anne will have finished university.
2 In 2016 Anne ______ around the world.
3 By 2018 Anne ______ work.
4 By 2020 Anne ______ a house.
5 In 2021 Anne ______ married.
6 By 2024 Anne ______ her first child.
7 By 2027 Anne ______ two children.
8 In 2055 Anne ______ from work.

3 Answer the questions about Anne's life plan using the future continuous or the future perfect.

1 Will she have finished university by 2016?
Yes, she will have finished university by 2016.
2 Will she be travelling around the world in 2018?
No, ______ in 2018.
3 Will she be starting work in 2017?
______ in 2017.
4 Will she have got married by 2020?
______ by 2020.
5 Will she have bought a house by 2022?
______ by 2022.
6 Will she be having her first child in 2025?
______ in 2025.
7 Will she have retired by 2050?
______ by 2050.

4 Complete the text about the future with the future perfect or the future continuous form of the verbs in brackets.

By 2050 technology will have taken over our lives and there will be no reason for us to leave our houses. We [1]______ (do) all our shopping on the internet and instead of visiting friends we [2]______ (chat) to them via our webcams. Many people [3]______ (work) from home in the future too, so cars will no longer be necessary.

As for our houses themselves, they [4]______ (grow) in size to incorporate giant solar panels. People [5]______ (throw away) their ovens and kitchen utensils in favour of a central robot to organize the family meals.

In 2050 everybody [6]______ (go) to exercise groups in their area to keep fit. The price of beauty treatments [7]______ (fall) considerably, so everybody [8]______ (look) good!

CHALLENGE!

Invent a life plan, and write some sentences about it.

An essay: for and against

Preparation

1 Read the task. Then put the paragraphs of the essay in the correct order.

'Rapid advances in technology will make the world of the future a more dangerous place.' Do you agree or disagree? Give reasons.

A To sum up, I do not think that technology will make the world more dangerous in the future. In my opinion, most of the dangers are based in fiction rather than fact.

B On the other hand, we can see that computers are already making the world a safer place in all kinds of different ways. For example, aeroplanes crash very rarely because computers can correct human error. Computer technology is also making cars safer.

C Technology is advancing quickly, particularly computer technology. As computers become more and more powerful, will they make the world safer or will they create new dangers?

D In science fiction films such as *I, Robot*, machines are usually portrayed as a dangerous threat to humans. In the real world, most scientists predict that computers will become more intelligent than humans, and so people naturally worry that we might not be able to control them.

1 ______ 2 ______ 3 ______ 4 ______

2

everybody scientists robots	be do have invent live be able to	for 150 years or more hours of free time most jobs faster computers cure every disease super-rich stop global warming

Use the chart to make predictions with *will*. Begin each sentence with *I think* or *I don't think*.

1 I don't think everybody will live for 150 years or more.
2 ______
3 ______
4 ______
5 ______
6 ______
7 ______

3 Underline and correct the mistake in some of these sentences. Tick the sentences that do not contain a mistake.

1 I think new diseases will emerge. ✓
2 Scientists will keep searching until they will find a cure. ______
3 Which cities will become uninhabitable when sea levels will rise? ______
4 Computers will become more intelligent than humans if science will keep advancing. ______
5 Governments will eventually ban carbon emissions, but it will be too late. ______
6 Global warming will get worse when more and more people in the world will have cars. ______
7 Will robots be our friends or will they try to take over the world? ______
8 Only very rich people will be able to afford cars when the oil will run out. ______

4 Read the task. Do you agree or disagree? Think of evidence to support your view and the opposite view.

'Science will make sure that life is better in the future.' Do you agree or disagree? Give reasons.

Opinion: I ______ with the statement.
Evidence supporting the opposite view: ______

Evidence supporting your view: ______

Writing task

5 In your notebook write an essay using your ideas from exercise 4. Use the Writing Bank on page 90 to help you. Write 200–250 words and follow the plan.

Paragraph 1 • introduction
Paragraph 2 • evidence supporting the opposite view
Paragraph 3 • evidence supporting your own view
Paragraph 4 • conclusion

Check your work

Have you

☐ used *will* correctly?
☐ written 200–250 words?
☐ checked grammar, spelling and punctuation?

SELF CHECK 5: GRAMMAR

1 **Complete the sentences using *will*, *may*, *might not* or *won't* and a verb in the box.**

be get go have like pass see win

1 We ________ to the theatre tonight. We've got some free tickets. (it's possible)
2 My brother had a terrible interview. He ________ the job. (I'm sure)
3 I ________ you at John's house. He's invited us both for dinner. (I'm sure)
4 They're a really good team, so we ________ the match. (it's possible)
5 That book is really boring. You ________ it. (I'm sure)
6 Jessica ________ time to do her homework tonight. She has to go out. (It's possible)
7 Don't wait for me. I ________ late. (it's possible)
8 You've studied a lot. You ________ all your exams. (I'm sure)

Your score /8

2 **Complete the first conditional sentences with the correct form of the verbs in brackets.**

1 If I ________ ill tomorrow, I ________ to school. (feel / not go)
2 If my sister ________ her driving test, my father ________ her a car. (pass / buy)
3 The police ________ us if they ________ our stolen car. (call / find)
4 If he ________ to work, he ________ any money. (not go / not earn)
5 I ________ it if I ________ it in my diary. (not remember / not write)
6 If we ________ late, our teacher ________ us into the class. (be / not let)
7 You ________ cold if you ________ a jacket. (get / not take)
8 We ________ if it ________ raining. (stay in / not stop)

Your score /16

3 **Complete these predictions with the future continuous or the future perfect of the verbs in brackets.**

1 In 10 years' time nobody ________ letters any more. (send)
2 In 20 years' time people ________ fewer cars. (buy)
3 In 30 years' time robots ________ teachers. (replace)
4 In 40 years' time tourists ________ holidays in space. (have)
5 In 50 years' time books ________. (disappear)
6 In 60 years' time all the world's rainforests ________. (go)
7 In 70 years' time the sea level ________ by 8 centimetres. (rise)
8 In 80 years' time people ________ on the moon. (live)

Your score /8

4 **Complete the second sentence with a pronoun and the future continuous or the future perfect. Use contractions in your answers.**

1 My father leaves his office at 5.30.
By 5.35 ________ his office.
2 The film starts at 8 o'clock tonight.
At 8.05 ________.
3 I'm doing my exams in May.
In May ________ my exams.
4 They're playing football at 11 o'clock on Saturday.
At 11.30 ________ football.
5 My little sister goes to bed at 9.30.
By 10 o'clock ________ to bed.
6 You're flying to Paris at 3.45 tomorrow afternoon.
At 4 o'clock ________ to Paris.
7 My mother leaves the house at 7 a.m. to drive to work.
At 7.05 ________ to work.
8 We're having the meeting tomorrow morning.
By 3 o'clock ________ the meeting.

Your score /8

Total /40

SELF CHECK 5: VOCABULARY

1 Complete the vocabulary quiz with words from Unit 5.

Quiz

1 It is important to invest in research so that scientists can continue to make important ________.

2 ________ species are at risk both from climate change and from people who kill the creatures for their skins or other body parts.

3 I get on really well with Sandra, but her friend Sophie has a really ________ sense of humour.

4 We need to ________ carbon emissions to save the planet.

5 ________ means there are too many people living in one place.

6 When the new gadget first went on sale, lots of parents ________ to the shops to buy them.

7 Doctors are hoping to ________ damaged body parts in the near future.

8 His condition is serious, but fortunately isn't thought to be ________.

9 Vets ________ sick animals.

10 Ever-faster ways are being introduced to ________ and share information.

11 Contrary to expectations, ________ devices such as washing machines didn't give women more time to relax.

12 It is impossible for anyone to fake their ID with ________ data, as we can't change our eyes or fingerprints.

13 Renewable energy such as ________ power and wind power is regarded as the only way forward.

14 World governments are introducing new measures to ________ climate change.

15 Scientists have found a hole in the ________ over the Arctic.

16 Another word for arms and legs is ________.

17 The biggest ________ on earth is in the Amazon.

18 The latest ________ in China has been an earthquake.

19 I was disappointed that the library couldn't ________ me with the information I needed.

20 My microwave is ________. Everything we put in it explodes.

Your score ____ /20

2 Choose the correct alternative.

Dear Sir or Madam,

I am writing to complain about my broadband internet connection. I am not satisfied with it because it is always [1] **misfunctioning / malfunctioning**.

The connection has not worked properly since it was set [2] **in / up**. It is difficult for me to [3] **get / obtain** online in the first place and when I do, the connection is frequently interrupted. You can imagine how difficult this makes things for me. As a student, I need to [4] **access / treat** information quickly and reliably. The fact that I cannot do so is not a fault of the search [5] **motor / engine** that I'm using.

However, it is not only the connection that concerns me. Yesterday, I received a bill from you for the wrong amount. I signed up with your internet service during a special offer, which I was told would be valid for the whole of this year. I [6] **did / made** a lot of research into prices and services before I contacted you, so I am hoping your sales staff [7] **gave / provided** me with the right information.

I am expecting you to solve the problems I have within the next week or I will terminate my contract with you. I have tried to [8] **reason / regenerate** with your customer services department by phone, without any success, and have spent a great deal of time, effort and money doing so. I am hoping that, as a gesture of goodwill, you will [9] **flock / reduce** my next bill and I also expect you to [10] **avoid / prevent** similar mistakes with my bill in the future.

Yours faithfully,

Lucy Edwards

Your score ____ /10

Total ____ /30

6 Telling tales

READING

Before reading: Crime

1 Match a noun from box A with a noun from box B to make new two-part nouns.

A	B
mountain	bed
book	research
flower	officer
market	case
police	bike

A	B
drain	table
hay	infection
coffee	fever
life	pipe
chest	guard

2 Complete the sentences with a two-part noun from exercise 1. There are two nouns that you do not need.

1 After the robbery, a police officer visited us.
2 The thief escaped by climbing down the ________.
3 He put the tray down on the ________.
4 Last weekend I went for a long ride on my new ________.
5 We asked the children not to walk on the ________.
6 She's not at work today because she's got a ________.
7 I always get ________ in the spring.
8 They're carrying out some ________ before launching the new product.

3 Complete the sentences with the past simple form of the verbs in the box.

admit ~~announce~~ convince deceive ignore investigate

1 The notice on the wall announced the disappearance of Jackie's dog.
2 Police ________ the murder of millionaire Jack Tremlin for over two years.
3 Luke ________ the jury that he was innocent.
4 Holly's grandmother ________ her family's requests that she should give up smoking.
5 The man who sold me the car ________ me into thinking it was new.
6 In the end, Amelia ________ she had stolen the money.

4 Read 'The Great Impostor' and complete the text with the missing sentences (a–f). There is one sentence that you do not need.

a During his life he had been, among other things, a civil engineer, a lawyer, a child-care expert, an editor, a cancer researcher and a teacher.
b He actually performed operations on wounded men, until news of one of his operations was printed in a Canadian newspaper.
c Most of his employers were satisfied with his work, until they discovered who he really was.
d After his third attempt to enter a Roman Catholic monastery, he joined the US army in 1941.
e After this episode, Demara sold his life story to *Life* magazine, which made him very well known.
f At one point he became so famous that a film was made about him called *The Great Impostor*, starring Tony Curtis.

The Great Impostor

The greatest impostor of all times is said to be Ferdinand Waldo Demara.

1 ________________

So who was this man, and why did he become so famous? Demara was born in Lawrence, Massachusetts, in 1921.

2 ________________

Unfortunately for Demara, he hated the army, but he managed to leave by borrowing the name of his army friend, Anthony Ignolia, and disappearing.

Demara used this technique of borrowing the names of people he'd met many times during his life. His most famous hoax was to pose as a surgeon, Joseph Cyr, on a Royal Canadian warship during the Korean War.

3 ________________ Cyr's mother read the article and informed the authorities that her son was, in fact, practising medicine in New Brunswick, Canada.

4 ________________. His new-found fame together with his enormous size (he was nearly two metres tall and had put on a lot of weight) meant that it was very difficult for him to find another job. Demara died at the age of 62 due to heart failure.

5 ________________. It is ironic that the only time he tried to act, in the horror film *The Hypnotic Eye*, he showed a complete lack of acting ability.

I'm your long-lost son

1 Complete the sentences with a word from the box.

> alleging announced confessed corroborate ~~drowned~~ jury overjoyed poverty precious sentenced sunk trial witnesses

1 Two people drowned _______ when a yacht hit some rocks yesterday.
2 The accused denied stealing the car, _______ that his brother had committed the crime.
3 The _______ voted unanimously in favour of a verdict of 'not guilty'.
4 My neighbour's son _______ that he had broken the window and offered to pay for the damage.
5 _______ has got worse since the beginning of the economic crisis.
6 Rescuers couldn't see the boat because it had already _______ to the bottom of the sea.
7 My father gave my mother a gold ring set with _______ stones for her birthday.
8 The head teacher _______ that he would be retiring the following year.
9 Two _______ stood up in court and said they had seen the criminal with blood on his hands.
10 The murderer was arrested last night. His _______ will be held next March.
11 The thief was _______ to six months in prison.
12 The police called the suspect's mother to _______ his story.
13 We were _______ at the news that we had won the million-pound prize.

Crime and punishment

2 Match the two halves of the sentences.

1 Police charged	a a unanimous verdict.
2 The suspect appeared	b evidence during the trial.
3 The defence lawyers tried to	c not gulity to all the charges.
4 Four witnesses gave	d him to a year in prison.
5 The accused pleaded	e a man with stealing my car.
6 The prosecution lawyers proved	f defend the accused.
7 The jury reached	g in court last week.
8 The judge sentenced	h the criminal was guilty.

3 Complete the puzzle to find the mystery word in the grey boxes.

1 The person that police have charged with the crime.
2 The decision reached by the jury in court.
3 To officially say that the accused is not guilty.
4 The person who decides on a suitable punishment.
5 A person who sees a crime.
6 To tell a criminal his punishment.
7 The place where a criminal appears.
8 People who try to prove the accused is guilty or innocent.

1	A	C	C	U	S	E	D					
					2							
	3											
			4									
	5											
			6									
					7							
	8											

Mystery word: _______

Negative prefixes

4 Use the words in the box with a negative prefix to complete the sentences.

> acceptable agreeable decisive honest ~~literate~~ mature relevant stable

1 Collette's grandfather can't read her letter because he's illiterate _______.
2 I always spend ages choosing what to wear because I'm so _______.
3 After he was caught stealing, my colleague lost his job for being _______.
4 Nobody believes my brother when he tells them his age because he's so _______.
5 We were really bored during the meeting because most of what the speaker said was _______.
6 My mother told my sister to leave the room because her behaviour was _______.
7 There was a very _______ atmosphere in class yesterday because Simon and Harry had just had a fight.
8 The builder refused to go up the ladder because it looked very _______.

GRAMMAR

Reported speech: statements

1 **Choose the correct alternatives.**

1 She told me this morning that she **was** / **is** going to the shops.
2 He told me last week that he **bought** / **had bought** an MP3 player.
3 They told us last month they **have** / **had** booked their summer holiday.
4 The teacher said yesterday she **will** / **would** give us a test soon.
5 Tom told me that he **can't** / **couldn't** come to dinner with us tomorrow.
6 My mum told me a long time ago that she **doesn't** / **didn't** enjoy driving in the town centre.
7 The newsreader said on tonight's news that there **were** / **had been** no victims in the crash.

2 **Rewrite the *say* sentences with *tell* and the *tell* sentences with *say*. Use pronouns where possible.**

1 She said to Sarah that she was going to bed.
She told her that she was going to bed ____.
2 He told Brad that he had bought some pizzas.
He said that he had bought some pizzas ____.
3 He told his sister that she was a great cook.
____.
4 My parents said to me that they were going to be late.
____.
5 We told our friends that they could come to our party.
____.
6 Lynn said to us that she didn't like dogs.
____.
7 I told my brother that I didn't want to go out.
____.
8 You said to me and Jimmy that you wanted to see us.
____.

3 **Rewrite the sentences in reported speech.**

1 'I did not rob the bank last month,' he said.
He said that he hadn't robbed the bank the month before.
2 'I was on holiday in Brazil until yesterday,' he told the policewoman.
____.
3 'You'll have to stay in jail tonight,' she told him.
____.
4 'I want to speak to my lawyer,' he told her.
____.
5 'You can see your lawyer tomorrow,' she said.
____.

4 **In 1925 the con man Victor Lustig succeeded in selling the Eiffel Tower to a French businessman, André Poisson. Read the reported conversation between the two men and write the direct speech.**

Lustig told Poisson that he was offering him an incredible bargain. He told him that he could sell him the Eiffel Tower. He said that the city could not afford to pay for the repairs any more. He told Poisson he would show him the Eiffel Tower the next day. Poisson said he wouldn't tell anyone about the deal. He told Lustig he wanted to pay for the tower that night. Lustig told Poisson that he couldn't live on his tiny salary and Poisson gave him some extra money. Lustig thanked Poisson and left the country with his money.

1 **Lustig:** 'I'm offering you an incredible bargain ____.'
2 **Lustig:** '____.'
3 **Lustig:** '____.'
4 **Lustig:** '____.'
5 **Poisson:** '____.'
6 **Poisson:** '____.'
7 **Lustig:** '____.'

CHALLENGE!

When was the last time you spoke to your grandparents? Report the conversation you had.

Investigating a crime in the home

1 Circle the word that does not belong.

1 cooker apron sink fridge
2 shower fireplace armchair sofa
3 chest of drawers lamp path wardrobe
4 basin stepladder mirror bath
5 flower bed hedge cupboard lawn
6 drainpipe balcony roof bookcase

2 Find thirteen house and garden words in the wordsearch. Answers may go down, across or diagonally.

Q	E	T	S	U	O	P	A	D	G	J	K	L	Z
X	C	V	B	O	N	C	O	O	K	E	R	M	W
R	Y	I	P	S	F	H	F	H	V	J	L	E	I
A	F	O	Q	X	Y	A	B	W	O	A	Q	F	M
R	E	U	S	V	I	L	O	A	B	A	S	I	N
M	M	I	S	W	X	B	M	R	A	U	A	E	R
C	G	I	R	T	B	E	O	D	L	A	M	P	P
H	A	Q	R	S	N	S	T	R	C	Z	E	A	P
A	G	R	J	R	H	I	W	O	O	K	E	T	I
I	V	U	P	S	O	E	L	B	N	Z	T	H	J
R	T	G	I	E	A	R	C	E	Y	J	U	M	S
Y	M	E	X	F	T	O	E	T	N	S	J	L	M
R	A	Y	B	O	O	K	C	A	S	E	U	J	K
C	U	P	B	O	A	R	D	R	E	O	G	Z	K

3 Rewrite the sentences with *must have*, *could have*, and *can't have*.

1 I'm sure Jill didn't forget about your birthday.
Jill can't have forgotten about your birthday.
2 Perhaps Catherine missed the bus.
______.
3 I'm sure Emma knew it was Friday.
______.
4 I'm sure Oliver didn't get the invitation.
______.
5 I'm sure Matt went to the doctor's.
______.
6 I'm sure Richard didn't have a basketball match.
______.
7 Perhaps Karen's car broke down.
______.

4 Look at the pictures. Use the words to write sentences with *must have*, *might have* and *can't have*.

1 John must / break his leg.
John must have broken his leg.
2 He might / fall off his bike.
______

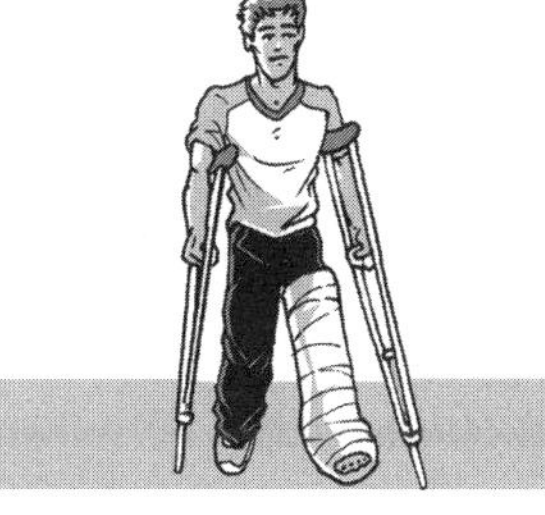

3 Rachel's friend must / write to her.
______

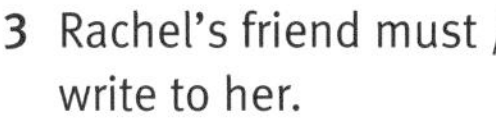

4 She might / ask her to go on holiday with her.
______

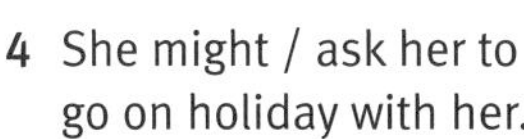

5 Their team can't / win.
______

6 They might / miss the match.
______

7 His car must / break down.
______
8 It can't / be a very good car.
______

CHALLENGE!

Sherlock Holmes is a very well-known fictional detective. Can you imagine him as a child? Invent information about him as a child using *must have*, *might have*, and *can't have*.

______

GRAMMAR

Reported speech: questions

1 **Complete the reported questions with the correct pronouns.**

1 He asked her if *she* could call *him* back.
2 Sally asked us if ______ could send her an email.
3 They asked ______ where I had seen their dog.
4 The teacher asked him if ______ would help you.
5 She asked ______ if I would go with ______ to the police.
6 I asked you what time ______ were picking me up.
7 We asked ______ when they would pay ______.

2 **Put the words in the correct order to make reported questions.**

1 me / been / he / had / where / asked / I
He asked me where I had been.
2 they / asked / come / them / if / could / we / for dinner
______.
3 asked / be / when / my car / I / ready / him / would
______.
4 I / the way / you / if / asked / knew / me
______.
5 going / her / asked / she / they / was / where
______.
6 he / a drink / him / wanted / asked / if / she
______.

3 **Look at the questions Simon's friends ask him when he goes back to school after a month. Then complete what Simon tells his mum that evening.**

1 **Sophie:** Where have you been?
2 **Abigail:** Did you go on holiday?
3 **Chloë:** Were you ill?
4 **Jessica:** Can you tell us about your trip?
5 **Ellie:** Does the head teacher know you're back?
6 **John:** Are you better?
7 **Emily:** Do you want to borrow my notes?
8 **Dan:** Will you still take your exams?
9 **Sam:** Why did you miss school?

1 Sophie asked *me where I'd been*.
2 Abigail asked ______.
3 Chloë ______.
4 Jessica ______.
5 Ellie ______.
6 John ______.
7 Emily ______.
8 Dan ______.
9 Sam ______.

4 **Read what Charlotte tells her friends about her interview for a part-time job. Then write the interview dialogue in direct speech.**

First the interviewer asked me which school I went to and [1] how old I was. Then she asked me [2] if I had ever had a job before. Next she asked me [3] what my best subject was at school and [4] if I had passed my last maths exam. After that she asked me [5] what I wanted to do when I left school and [6] if I was planning to go to university. Finally, she asked me [7] if I would work two evenings during the week and [8] if I could start the next week.

1 '*How old are you*?'
2 '______?'
3 '______?'
4 '______?'
5 '______?'
6 '______?'
7 '______?'
8 '______?'

CHALLENGE!

Think of some difficult questions you have asked a friend recently.

I asked ______
______
I asked ______
______

Think of some difficult questions your friends have asked you recently.

______ asked me ______
______
______ asked me ______
______

A formal letter: making a reservation

Preparation

1 Complete the sentences with the words in the box.

confirm grateful mind possible

1 Would you ________ sending me further details of the bus service?
2 I would be ________ if you could send me payment details for our stay.
3 Would it be ________ to have a triple room for the three of us?
4 Please can you ________ that we will be collected from the village?

2 Complete the letter with the polite requests from exercise 1.

Dear Mr King,

Further to our telephone conversation yesterday morning, I am writing to confirm that I wish to make a reservation for myself and two friends for the weekend of 3rd–5th July.

1 ______________________________

We would also like to express our preference for a room with a balcony, so that we can sit outside. On the telephone you mentioned an airport bus which passes through the village nearest the hotel. 2 ______________________________, so that we can plan our journey?

Finally, 3 ______________________________ I will send you a cheque for the deposit by post as soon as you confirm the amount.

I look forward to hearing from you in due course.

Yours sincerely,

Bethany R. Simpson

Ms B. R. Simpson

PS 4 ______________________________

We will be arriving some time on Friday evening, depending on the bus service.

3 Rewrite the informal phrases with a formal phrase from the letter.

1 After our phone call
Further to our telephone conversation.
2 I want to book a room
______________________________.
3 We want a room with a balcony
______________________________.
4 Hope to hear from you soon
______________________________.
5 Best wishes
______________________________.

4 Put the words in order to make sentences with two objects.

1 you / send / a brochure / can / me
______________________________?
2 gave / roses / her / he / some
______________________________.
3 sent / deposit / them / I / the
______________________________.
4 meal / cooked / she / a / him
______________________________.
5 lie / me / told / a / you
______________________________.

Writing task

5 In your notebook write a formal letter to make a reservation for yourself and five friends for the adventure weekend advertised below. Use the Writing Bank on page 91 to help you. Write 150–200 words and include the following:

- polite requests to ask for
  - three rooms for two people on the same floor
  - directions by car to the hotel
  - payment details for the weekend
  - more information about the activities
- an extra comment at the end of your letter after your name.

A weekend with a difference

Come alone or with friends to enjoy the Westerfield Wild Weekend. An experience you'll never forget! Bungee jumping from Basilton Bridge, paintballing in the park, hang-gliding from the highest hill and much, much more!

Phone The Westerfield Hotel
03927 391 for more information

Check your work

Have you
- ☐ started and finished your letter appropriately?
- ☐ organized your letter into paragraphs?
- ☐ written 150–200 words?
- ☐ checked grammar, spelling and punctuation?

SELF CHECK 6: GRAMMAR

1 Write the sentences in reported speech.

1 'I work in a hospital.'
She said ______________________________.

2 'I'm busy tomorrow.'
Andy said ______________________________.

3 'We've finished our homework.'
They told me ______________________________.

4 'I ate too much yesterday.'
Helen said ______________________________.

5 'I'll call you next week.'
He told his grandmother ______________________________.

6 'We can stay out late tonight.'
They said ______________________________.

7 'I don't like Chinese food.'
She said ______________________________.

8 'I'm going home.'
She told us ______________________________.

Your score ___ **/8**

2 Complete the sentences with the correct form of *say* or *tell*.

1 He ________ me he was tired.
2 She ________ she was ill.
3 We didn't ________ our parents about the accident.
4 Did you ________ him the meeting was cancelled?
5 Gina ________ she didn't like eggs.
6 Mark didn't ________ what time he was coming.
7 I ________ you it was late.
8 The man ________ he was a police officer.
9 Did he ________ you his phone number?
10 What did they ________ to you?

Your score ___ **/10**

3 Complete the reported questions.

1 I ________ you if you could hear me.
2 He asked them ________ they wanted a drink.
3 They asked me ________ I lived.
4 She asked ________ if we had understood.
5 We asked her if she ________ disappointed.
6 I asked her ________ she was doing.
7 He asked us if we ________ enjoying the film.
8 They asked ________ where he had been.

Your score ___ **/8**

4 Write reported questions.

1 'Do you have a car?'
He asked me ______________________________.

2 'What sports do you play?'
The doctor asked him ______________________________.

3 'Are you in a hurry?'
I asked my father ______________________________.

4 'Have you cleaned your shoes?'
She asked him ______________________________.

5 'Where did you park your car?'
I asked her ______________________________.

6 'Can you drive?'
She asked me ______________________________.

7 'What are you listening to?'
We asked him ______________________________.

8 'What will you do with the prize money?'
They asked us ______________________________.

Your score ___ **/8**

5 Look at the incorrect reported statements and questions. Write the sentences correctly.

1 My brother **told** he was going out.
______________________________.

2 We asked them where they **are** going.
______________________________.

3 I asked **she** if she had a pen.
______________________________.

4 My uncle said he **doesn't enjoy** our trip to Monaco.
______________________________.

5 Her parents **said** her she had to work harder.
______________________________.

6 They asked me **did** I **want** to help.
______________________________.

Your score ___ **/6**

Total ___ **/40**

SELF CHECK 6: VOCABULARY

1 Complete the vocabulary quiz with words from Unit 6.

Quiz

1 She put her clothes away in the ________ in her bedroom.
2 The ________ reached a verdict of 'not guilty'.
3 My grandmother spends all day sitting in her favourite ________ doing the crossword.
4 He looked over towards the fireplace, and realized that the clock wasn't in its usual place on the ________.
5 My father's out in the garden cutting the ________ which goes around our garden.
6 My parents were ________ when I passed my final exams.
7 Although he was as clever as the other students, his behaviour was very ________ for his age.
8 Although he had earned a fortune, at the end of his life he died in ________.
9 They ________ to writing the graffiti as soon as the police officer came into the room.
10 The suspect is being kept at the police station until his ________ next week.
11 You'll need a ________ to reach the top shelf.
12 The man was ________ to pay a £5000 fine.
13 The prosecution lawyers had enough ________ to prove him guilty.
14 I pulled back the ________ to see if it was raining.
15 I don't know why, but I have an ________ fear of spiders.
16 His sister had been a ________ to the crime, but she didn't want to give evidence in court.
17 The company ________ that they would be making a number of redundancies.
18 She can't make the dinner because her ________ isn't working.
19 We were very ________ with the service at the restaurant and so we didn't leave a tip.
20 She really must do something about her handwriting. It's ________.

Your score ____ /20

2 Complete the text with the correct words (a–d).

A rather unusual vandal appeared in [1]________ last week in Rockenhausen, Germany. The [2]________ was an 89-year-old grandmother who had been slashing the tyres of cars parked outside her house. Police [3]________ her with vandalism after a [4]________ saw her damaging the vehicles. Mrs Kohl [5]________ guilty to the charges, claiming that she had wanted to put people [6]________ parking in her road. She alleged that it was [7]________ for residents to find a safe place to cross the road and she was fed up [8]________ the situation. After the jury reached their [9]________, Mrs Kohl was ordered to pay a large fine. However, Mrs Kohl pointed out to the court that she had no money for the fine, and she requested an alternative punishment. Finally, the judge [10]________ her to knit jumpers for all of her victims instead.

	a	b	c	d
1	a trial	b hearing	c court	d police station
2	a accused	b lawyer	c judge	d admitted
3	a arrested	b charged	c detained	d accused
4	a observer	b member	c someone	d witness
5	a said	b pleaded	c admitted	d told
6	a on	b away	c off	d through
7	a immature	b impractical	c impossible	d impatient
8	a off	b on	c to	d with
9	a verdict	b evidence	c sentence	d confession
10	a acquitted	b sentenced	c charged	d accused

Your score ____ /10

Total ____ /30

7 Friendship

READING

Before reading: Making friends

1 Complete the sentences with the words and phrases in the box.

an obligation close to my heart genuine interrupt ~~judge~~ nothing in common on the go

1 It's dangerous to judge ____________ people by their appearance.
2 My music collection is my most important possession. It's very ____________.
3 It's almost ____________ to invite all your relatives to your wedding.
4 Is that painting a ____________ Picasso?
5 Please don't ____________ me when I'm talking on the phone.
6 We lost touch because we had ____________.
7 I'm sorry. I've been ____________ all day and I forgot to call you.

2 Read the text and match the headings (1–6) with the paragraphs (A–E). There is one heading that you do not need.

1 Rediscover books and the art of reading
2 Take a walk around a supermarket
3 Go back to traditional fun
4 Get out your writing paper
5 Match a voice to a name
6 Go to other people's homes

Life without the internet

Recently, an earthquake in Taiwan destroyed internet lines in Asia, upsetting the lives of millions of people dependent on the web for their work and social relationships. Here are some hints on how to cope if a similar situation occurs where you live.

A ____________

With no chatrooms or games sites, you'll have to find your own entertainment. Take out the games boards you put away when you were given your first PC and play Monopoly or Cluedo with your friends and family. You'll be surprised at how much fun it is.

B ____________

Instead of emailing your friends, you'll have to talk to them on the phone. And perhaps you can get to know some of the many friends you made in the chatroom and find out if they're actually anything like they said they were in their profiles.

C ____________

As an alternative to picking up the phone, you could visit your friends in their own houses, instead of chatting to them every night from your room. That way you could find things to do together and maybe meet their families. You will also be burning off calories, which will help keep you fit and healthy.

D ____________

The art of letter-writing died with the advent of the internet, and with it, the joy of receiving letters from others. Write some letters to your friends in foreign countries, and experience the pleasure of getting a letter back.

E ____________

Discover where your local library is and remind yourself what research was like before the age of the online search. Remember, many others will be doing the same as you, so it will be an ideal meeting place for people of your age.

VOCABULARY

Is there such a thing as a true friend?

1 **Replace the words in bold with a synonym.**

1 When my Dad's telling us off, he won't tolerate anyone **speaking when he's speaking**. interrupting
2 I'm exhausted! I've been **busy** all day! ________
3 You could see the **worry** on her face when she heard about her friend's accident. ________
4 I thought the exam had gone very well, but my teacher thought **in a different way**. ________
5 He caught a **view** of his friends in the playground as he was taken to the head teacher's office. ________
6 It was such a nice day that we **walked** through the park **without hurrying**. ________
7 When you are a small child you don't have any **things you have to do**. ________
8 The only thing I have **the same as** my brother is a love of animals. ________
9 Sara always **forms an opinion about** people before she really knows them. ________
10 She has no experience with children, so she doesn't know how to **behave towards** the new baby. ________
11 My mother is a poet, so literature is very **important to me**. ________
12 The painting they found in her attic was a **real** Picasso. ________
13 They became close when he offered her **sympathy** after her father died. ________
14 Many public buildings have been adapted to provide access for **carriages for disabled people**. ________
15 There was a **loud** crash as the lorry hit the wall. ________

Three-part phrasal verbs

2 **Complete the sentences with the correct form of a verb in the box.**

not come cut fall get ~~not get~~ put look not look

1 They never play together because they don't get on with each other.
2 My sister's depressed because she ________ out with her best friend last week.
3 Nobody saw Rick sending text messages in class, so he ________ away with it.
4 I'm trying to lose weight, so I ________ down on sweets and chocolates this month.
5 We ________ up with Harry's music for long enough, so we asked him to turn it off.
6 Her older brothers and sisters ________ down on her until she got a better job.
7 She ________ up with the idea herself. She copied it from another student.
8 My family ________ up to me until I qualified as a lawyer.

3 **Complete the sentences with the rest of the phrasal verb and a pronoun.**

1 I'm not talking to my sister because I've fallen out with her.
2 Our new neighbours think they're better than us. They're always looking ______ ______ ______.
3 Amy had a great idea for Tamara's present. I'm really glad she came ______ ______ ______.
4 There's nothing she can do about her mother-in-law, so she'll have to put ______ ______ ______.
5 You're eating too much fat. You need to cut ______ ______ ______.
6 Lily always sits next to Maggie because she gets ______ well ______ ______.
7 Simon's little brother will do anything Simon says because he really looks ______ ______ ______.
8 The teacher saw Oliver cheating in the exam, so he didn't get ______ ______ ______.

-ed / *-ing* adjectives

4 **Complete the sentences with the correct form of an adjective in the box.**

annoyed/ing bored/ing depressed/ing fascinated/ing exhausted/ing entertained/ing frightened/ing ~~interested/ing~~

1 I'm not very interested in politics.
2 He gave a brilliant talk. We were all ________.
3 They screamed all the way through the film. It was very ________.
4 I watched a really good TV programme last night. It was very ________.
5 We were so ________ during the meeting that we nearly fell asleep.
6 This weather is so ________. I wish it would stop raining!
7 My little brother is really ________. He's always asking questions.
8 I've had a really busy day and I'm absolutely ________.

Comparatives and superlatives

1 Complete the sentences with the comparative or superlative form of the adverbs in brackets.

1 Connor cooks better ______ than Ed, but Oscar cooks ______ of the three. (well)
2 Phoebe walks ______ than Alice, but Keira walks ______ of the three. (fast)
3 Ed dances ______ than Oscar, but Connor dances ______. (energetically)
4 Alice works ______ than Keira, but Phoebe works ______. (hard)
5 Oscar speaks ______ than Connor, but Ed speaks ______. (clearly)
6 Keira drives ______ than Phoebe, but Alice drives ______. (carefully)

2 Look at the results of the competition and complete the sentences with the correct form of the adjectives and adverbs in the brackets.

	TOM	JAY	ALAN	DAN
QUALITIES				
Strength	7	10	8	9
Intelligence	10	7	9	8
Patience	9	8	10	7
SKILLS				
Running	8	9	7	10
Writing	10	8	9	7
Parking	7	9	8	10

1 Tom runs faster ______ than Alan. (fast)
2 Dan is ______ than Jay. (patient)
3 Dan writes ______ of the four. (accurately)
4 Alan is ______ than Tom. (strong)
5 Dan parks ______ of them all. (well)
6 Jay doesn't park ______ Dan. (well)
7 Jay is ______ of them all. (intelligent)
8 Alan runs ______ of them all. (fast)
9 Jay writes ______ than Alan. (correctly)
10 Dan isn't ______ Tom. (intelligent)

3 Complete the sentences with a phrase from the box to make comparisons.

as it was when I bought it | she was as a child | than five years ago | than he used to be | than it used to be | than I was before

1 My brother's more confident ______.
2 This watch isn't as accurate ______.
3 She's slimmer than ______.
4 I'm happier in my new job ______.
5 Fewer people drive their cars in the centre now ______.
6 This jacket is less trendy ______.

4 Use the words to make superlative sentences with the present perfect.

1 She / interesting / person / I / ever / meet.
She's the most interesting person I've ever met.
2 That / exciting / film / I / ever / see.
______
3 This / unreliable / car / we / ever / buy.
______
4 He's / funniest / man / I / ever / work with.
______
5 That / expensive / present / he / ever / receive.
______
6 That / nice / thing / you / ever / say.
______
7 That / good / meal / I / ever / eat.
______

CHALLENGE!

Use some of the qualities and skills in the chart in exercise 2 and add some of your own to write six sentences about yourself in relation to your classmates.

Relationships

1 **Complete the sentences that describe the speech bubbles with the past simple form of a verb in the box. (sb = somebody)**

back sb up ~~confide in sb~~ fall out with sb
keep in touch with sb lend sb a hand
let sb down make up with sb put up with sb

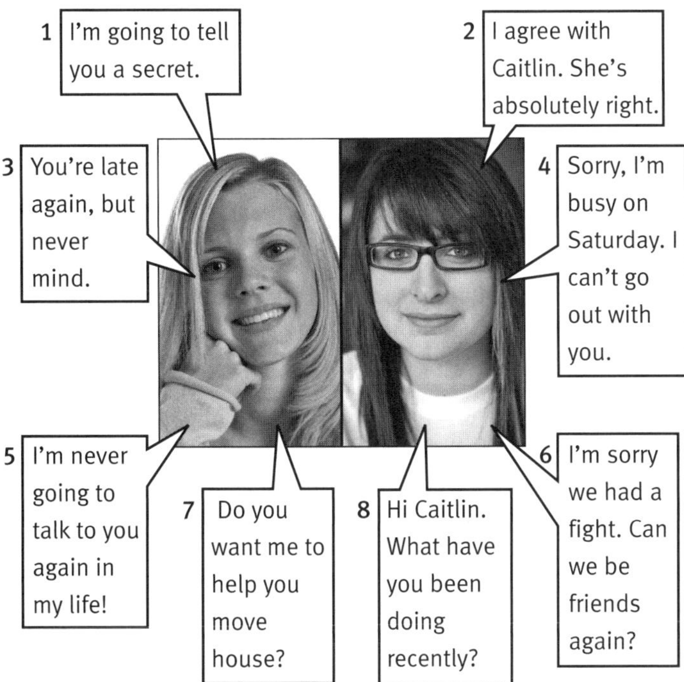

1 Caitlin *confided in* Nicole.
2 Nicole ________ Caitlin ________ in the discussion.
3 Caitlin ________ Nicole although she was always late.
4 Nicole ________ Caitlin ________ on Saturday night.
5 Caitlin ________ Nicole.
6 They soon ________ after their argument.
7 Caitlin ________ Nicole ________ to move house.
8 Nicole ________ Caitlin after she moved.

2 **Match the beginnings of the sentences (1–7) with the endings (a–g).**

1 My brother's started hanging — c
2 Did you lose
3 Ryan's big brother always stands
4 My best friend let
5 Helen fell
6 I get
7 My parents put

a me down last night.
b out with Anisa over a game of chess.
c out with some boys in another class.
d up for him if he gets in a fight.
e on really well with my cousins.
f up with us because they love us.
g touch with your friends when you left school?

3 **Rewrite the sentences with a phrase from the box in a suitable tense.**

~~confide in sb~~ fall out with sb get on well with sb
hang out with sb lose touch with sb make up
put up with sb stand up for sb

1 I don't often **tell my secrets** to anyone.
I don't often confide in anyone.
2 My brother **has always had a good relationship** with my father.
________.
3 Alan **had an argument with** Oliver during the football match.
________.
4 We **spent some time** together in the park yesterday before going home.
________.
5 They used to be friends, but they **stopped seeing each other** when they started work.
________.
6 My sister **supported me** in our last family argument.
________.
7 We**'ve tolerated** our neighbours for long enough.
________.
8 I called my friend and tried to **end my disagreement** with her.
________.

CHALLENGE!

Write about a friendship you have with a good friend.

Second conditional

1 Join the two sentences to make one sentence using the second conditional.

1 You go to bed late. You feel bad in the morning.
If you didn't go to bed late, you wouldn't feel bad in the morning.

2 You don't put your clothes away. Your room is a mess.
______________________.

3 You don't go shopping. There isn't any food in the fridge.
______________________.

4 You're always with your friends. You don't have time for me.
______________________.

5 You don't study. You don't pass your exams.
______________________.

6 You eat a lot of sweets. You've got toothache.
______________________.

7 You don't go to football practice. You aren't in the football team.
______________________.

2 Complete the sentences with the past simple or *would* + base form.

Mother

1 If only I *had* more time. (have)

2 I wish you ________ to me. (listen)

3 If only you ________ more helpful. (be)

4 I never know where you're going. I wish you ________ me. (tell)

5 I wish we ________ so badly. (not get on)

Daughter

6 If only you ________ so busy. (not be)

7 I wish you ________. (relax)

8 You're always angry with me. I wish you ________ at me all the time. (not shout)

9 I wish you ________ me alone. (leave)

10 If only I ________ at home. (not live)

3 Use the words to write complete sentences.

1 I / rather / you / not turn / the TV on
I'd rather you didn't turn the TV on.

2 I / rather / stay / in a hotel / than in a tent
______________________.

3 I / wish / we / live / in a bigger house
______________________.

4 If only / we / see / more of each other
______________________.

5 If / you / not / work so much / you / be / happier
______________________.

6 I / rather / we / go / for a walk
______________________.

7 If only / you / be / ten years younger
______________________.

4 Read the dialogue and complete the spaces with the correct form of the verb in brackets or *would* + the base form.

Father If you've got a couple of minutes, I [1] *'d like* to have a talk. (like)
Jake Why? What's wrong?
Father I don't like the people you hang out with.
Jake I wish you [2] ________ that. (not say)
Father They aren't good for you.
Jake Why? What's the problem?
Father I've told you before. If only you [3] ________ to me! (listen)
Jake What? They're older than me?
Father Yes. And they're a bad influence. I'd rather you [4] ________ seeing them. (stop)
Jake I wish you [5] ________ to them sometimes. (speak)
Father I don't need to speak to them. I know what they're like.
Jake If you [6] ________ to know them, I'm sure you [7] ________ them. (get / like)
Father I'd rather not [8] ________ to know them, thank you. (get)
Jake But, they're my friends!
Father Well, I wish you [9] ________ some new friends. (make)

CHALLENGE!

Think of your friends and family. Would you like anyone's behaviour to change? Write four sentences using *wish*, *if only*, and *I'd rather* and the second conditional.

____
____
____
____

Emails to apologize

Preparation

1 Look at the phrases used for apologizing. Mark them F (formal) or I (informal).

1 I'm ever so sorry for being so moody. I
2 Please accept my apologies for spoiling your meal. ___
3 I'm sorry, but I had been asleep and I hadn't really woken up properly. ___
4 I'm really, really sorry for not remembering your birthday. ___
5 I am writing to apologize for being so rude at the weekend. ___
6 I am terribly sorry about the damage I caused. ___
7 I'm very sorry for shouting at you yesterday. ___
8 I very much regret leaving my bike in such an unsuitable place. ___

2 Complete each email with two of the phrases from exercise 1.

Dear Mrs Summers,

[1] ________________. I am extremely embarrassed about my behaviour and I hope you can forgive me for leaving your house in such a hurry.

The reason I had to go was because a friend had called me telling me he had had an accident, and he needed me to take him to hospital. You had made such an effort to prepare a delicious meal that I should have at least explained to you why I had to leave in the middle of lunch.

I have recently discovered that you were very upset after I left, and that nobody felt like eating lunch. I would like to invite you to dinner at the restaurant of your choice to compensate for my thoughtlessness. I am available all next week, so perhaps you would like to suggest a day which would be convenient for you.

[2] ________________. I hope you understand that this was not my intention.

Yours sincerely

Bruno Rivers

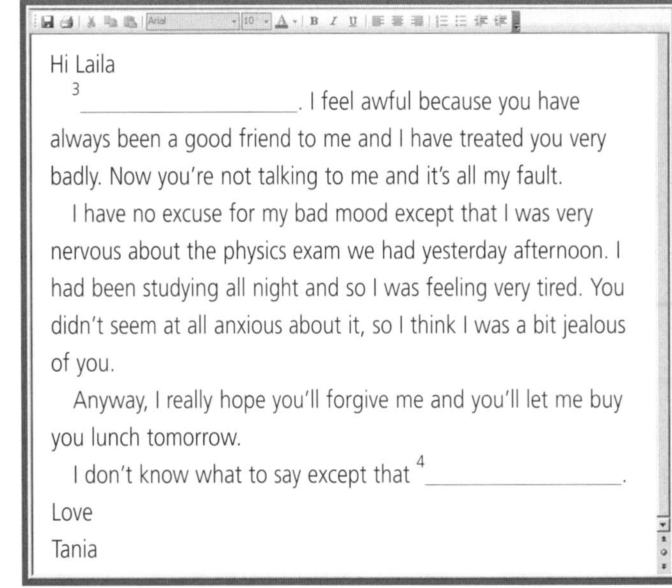

Hi Laila

[3] ________________. I feel awful because you have always been a good friend to me and I have treated you very badly. Now you're not talking to me and it's all my fault.

I have no excuse for my bad mood except that I was very nervous about the physics exam we had yesterday afternoon. I had been studying all night and so I was feeling very tired. You didn't seem at all anxious about it, so I think I was a bit jealous of you.

Anyway, I really hope you'll forgive me and you'll let me buy you lunch tomorrow.

I don't know what to say except that [4] ________________.

Love

Tania

3 Underline the correct time preposition.

1 Would you like to come to dinner **on** / **in** Sunday?
2 The party starts **on** / **at** 9.30.
3 The ceremony will be held **on** /**at** Friday 23rd May.
4 We're going to stay out late **on** / **at** night.
5 I'm going to celebrate **on** / **at** the weekend.
6 The tour will start early **in** / **on** the morning.
7 Let's go on holiday together **on** / **in** the summer.
8 We went to Australia **on** / **in** 2000.

Writing task

4 In your notebook, write an email for each of the following situations:

1 An email to a friend to apologize for getting angry about something unimportant.
2 An email to an adult to apologize for causing an accident.

Use the Writing Bank on pages 90 and 91 to help you. Invent the following information for the emails:

- how you feel now
- what exactly happened
- what you're going to do next.

Check your work

Have you

- [ ] used the appropriate register for each email?
- [ ] used time prepositions correctly?
- [ ] included all the information from the task?
- [ ] started and finished your email appropriately?
- [ ] checked grammar, spelling and punctuation?

SELF CHECK 7: GRAMMAR

1 Rewrite the words in bold without changing the meaning. Use the correct form of the word in brackets and any other appropriate words.

1 The journey is **less fast** by train than by car. (slow)

____

2 You should drive **more carefully**. (dangerous)

____

3 It was the **easiest** exam I've ever done. (difficult)

____

4 We stayed in the **least clean** hotel in the world. (dirty)

____

5 She wants to have a **more relaxed** life. (stressful)

____

6 Dan has a **less loud** voice than Pete. (quiet)

____

7 He's a lot **more confident** than he used to be. (shy)

____

8 Patricia **doesn't paint badly**. (good)

____

9 Her house **isn't as near to** the park **as** ours. (far)

____

10 People often walk **less slowly** in a city than in the countryside. (fast)

____

Your score /10

2 Complete the text with comparative or superlative form of the adjectives in brackets.

I've just been visiting a friend in the countryside. Everything is so different there. It's a lot [1] ________ (green) than my town, of course. People say that life's [2] ________ ________ (noisy) in the countryside, but I don't agree. The birds were so loud they woke me up! It's certainly [3] ________ ________ (crowded) in a village than in a big town, and yes – towns are [4] ________ ________ (polluted) because of all the cars. But I find the people in my town [5] ________ (friendly), probably because I know so many of them. Actually, the people in my region are considered to be the [6] ________ ________ (unfriendly) people in the whole country. And my friend's neighbour was [7] ________ ________ (rude) man I've ever met in my life. And another thing: is the countryside really [8] ________ (safe) than a town? I don't think so. You have to drive much [9] ________ ________ (careful) down those country roads because there might be a big tractor coming at you round the corner.

I love spending holidays in the country, but I think I'll be living in my town for a bit [10] ________ (long).

Your score /10

3 Choose the correct verb.

1 If you **worry** / **worried** less, you **would have** / **had** an easier life.

2 We **would** / **had** go to the party if they **invited** / **invite** us.

3 What **would** / **did** you do if you **won** / **'d win** the prize?

4 If she **wouldn't** / **didn't** like fish, she **didn't** / **wouldn't** eat it.

5 If I **had** / **would have** the choice, I **had** / **would** live near the sea.

6 Karen **would sing** / **sang** for you if you **'d ask** / **asked** her.

7 Many people **wouldn't** / **didn't** eat hamburgers if they **weren't** / **didn't be** so cheap.

8 I **'d come** / **came** with you if I **could** / **did can** swim.

9 It **was** / **would be** strange if you **wouldn't be** / **weren't** here next year.

10 We **'d** / **'ll** all be healthier if we **ate** / **'d eat** more fruit and vegetables.

Your score /10

4 Add *wish*, *only* or *rather*.

Ryan What shall we do today?

Jack I got a new computer game for my birthday. We could play that.

Amy I'd [1] ________ be outside. It's a lovely day.

Ryan Yes, it is. If [2] ________ we had a boat. We could go sailing.

Jack Do you know how to sail?

Ryan No, but it looks so exciting. I [3] ________ someone would teach me.

Amy I [4] ________ we were by the sea now. If [5] ________ we all lived at the seaside.

Jack Why don't we go to the lake in the park and watch the boats? We could take a picnic. My mum's got some leftover chicken and salad, and I got lots of chocolate for my birthday ...

Amy I [6] ________ you wouldn't keep talking about food. Your house is miles away. If [7] ________ the shop round the corner was open.

Ryan I'd [8] ________ get something at the café in the park.

Amy So would I. But the café's expensive. I [9] ________ we had a bit more money.

Jack I got some money for my birthday. If [10] ________ I'd brought it with me!

Your score /10

Total /40

SELF CHECK 7: VOCABULARY

1 Complete the vocabulary quiz with words from Unit 7.

Quiz

1 My father used to be a farmer, so rural issues have always been ________.
2 We went to a ________ talk about local history. I didn't want it to end.
3 I try to ________ salt by not putting any on my food, but there's a lot of it in processed foods.
4 She's very loyal, and always ________ you, even if she thinks you're wrong.
5 Please try not to ________ people when they are speaking. Wait for your turn.
6 Everyone's ________ all the time these days. It's about time we all relaxed a bit.
7 I used to ________ my older brother, as he seemed to know so much about everything.
8 He's pretended to be ill so often that it's difficult to know if this illness is ________.
9 She goes away somewhere sunny from time to time to lift her spirits, as she finds the cold and damp weather ________.
10 I've had enough. I can't ________ his moods any longer.
11 It's really sad when you want to be friends with someone who doesn't want to ________ you.
12 We all thought the show was ________. We didn't stop laughing from start to finish and the time flew by.
13 They stopped being friends because they realized that they had nothing ________.
14 After playing with my little nephew and niece all afternoon, I was ________.
15 We spent ages trying to think of an original present to buy him, but we didn't ________ anything.
16 Restaurants like this ________ serving poor food because nobody complains.
17 I didn't see the person clearly. I just caught a ________ of a girl walking away.
18 It's silly to ________ someone over a little thing when you could just talk about it and clear it up.
19 The response was unanimous: a ________ 'no' to the new housing development.
20 Some people don't like to ________ others, and prefer to keep their troubles to themselves.

Your score /20

2 Complete the text with the correct words, (a–d).

Many people have used websites such as Friends Reunited to get back in touch with old school friends or workmates. I don't really see why I'd want to contact people that I didn't particularly [1] ________ with all those years ago. I think it's only natural that, when you move on in life, you [2] ________ with people. What's changed is that we now have the technology to do something about it. This is a subject that's quite close to my [3] ________, as my sister had a difficult experience. She contacted her childhood best friend and when she found out she lived nearby, she was really pleased. 'I [4] ________ with her over a stupid argument, and I always regretted it,' she said. 'We'd always had a lot [5] ________, and I never really found anyone to replace her. When we met up again, I was really pleased when I saw her [6] ________ towards me. We talked and talked. She [7] ________ me about her life troubles, and I offered her a [8] ________ to cry on. We started meeting up regularly, and I was so happy. Then she suddenly stopped contacting me, and wouldn't answer my calls. I couldn't understand why she didn't want to [9] ________ with me any more. I was so [10] ________, both with her and myself, for getting involved again.'

1 a get over b get on c put up d stand up
2 a put up b hang out c look up d lose touch
3 a heart b shoulder c concern d judge
4 a fell out b made up c came up d cut down
5 a obligations b otherwise c in common d on the go
6 a treating b sauntering c resounding d interrupting
7 a backed b stood up for c confided in d looked down on
8 a wheelchair b heart c glimpse d shoulder
9 a hang out b fall out c get away d lose touch
10 a amused b annoyed c entertaining d depressing

Your score /10

Total /30

8 Travel

READING

Before reading: In the wild

1 Complete the text with the words in the box.

~~claws~~ horn thrive tusks

I saw an artificial tiger rug recently. It was very realistic, right down to its sharp-looking [1] claws ______. It reminded me of the huge number of animals in the wild that are killed for profit. Many elephants are killed for their [2] __________, which are used to make medicines and other remedies in some parts of the world. Rhinoceros [3] __________ is used for the same purpose, and, although the practice is illegal, it continues to [4] __________. It is such a shame that the hunters don't see the power and beauty of these animals.

2 Read the text. Are the sentences true or false? Write T or F.

1. The writer didn't have to pay for the trip. ____
2. There were eight volunteers staying at the centre. ____
3. The volunteers had to rescue the animals from cruel owners. ____
4. They had to feed the animals immediately after breakfast. ____
5. The volunteers entered some of the cages to feed the animals. ____
6. They didn't open the enclosures of the big cats. ____
7. The writer thinks that gap years are character-building, but don't help you academically. ____

An unforgettable experience

The trip of my lifetime was definitely the month I spent in Ecuador on an animal rescue project in my gap year. I'd worked temping for six months to finance my trip, and I had the most amazing time imaginable.

I stayed with eight other volunteers in the Santa Martha Rescue Centre, which is situated in a rural part of the Andes, surrounded by volcanoes. The centre cares for animals that have been treated badly by their owners and range from jaguars and pumas to monkeys and parrots. Our job was to feed the animals and keep them clean.

A typical day started at 7 a.m. when we had to give the animals their breakfast before having our own. After breakfast we helped the local staff with maintenance jobs around the centre, like repairing cages and building new enclosures. We normally stopped at around 2 p.m. and then went back to feed the animals again at 4 p.m.

I spent most of my time chopping fruit for the animals, but the best bit was entering the cages and feeding them. My favourites were the baby monkeys who greeted me each morning by jumping all over me and pulling my hair. Watering the young cats was slightly more dangerous and we had to do it in pairs. One person would entertain the cats while the other opened the cages and grabbed the water bowls. We filled the adults' bowls from outside the enclosure, which seemed like a much more sensible idea to me.

The whole trip was unforgettable, and I would recommend everyone to take a gap year. You gain confidence and become more self-sufficient as well as getting hands-on experience of your degree subject. Just earn some money, book the trip you fancy most and get out there and do it!

Big cat diary

1 Complete the sentences with the words in the box.

awesome boast cross hurtle ~~markings~~ nocturnal plain soaked springs stealthy stroll thumping trail trundling trunk

1 The markings on a tiger's coat help it to hide in the long grass.
2 There was a storm while we were playing football, so we got ________.
3 From the top of the hill we had a great view of the ________. We could see for miles!
4 I don't like people who ________ about their achievements all the time.
5 Kevin doesn't like the ________ way his boss is always walking around the office.
6 An elephant uses its ________ to put food in its mouth.
7 My mother was quite ________ when I lost my new coat.
8 Rockets ________ through space these days at speeds of nearly 30,000 kilometres per hour.
9 My little brother gives me a terrible fright every time he ________ out from behind the door to surprise me.
10 Some wild animals sleep during the day because they are ________.
11 We couldn't drive very fast because there was a big lorry ________ along in front of us.
12 We walked along the ________ until we came to a gate which led out onto the road.
13 After escaping from the wild dog, my heart was ________ fast.
14 We had a great time at the theme park. One of the rides was absolutely ________.
15 Yesterday we decided to ________ around the old part of town, looking at the sights.

Verbs and prepositions

2 Match the two parts of the sentences.

1 We aren't waiting
2 The train had already left when we arrived
3 I felt uncomfortable. They were all staring
4 He couldn't help boasting
5 I apologized to her
6 She argued
7 My uncle insisted
8 This isn't my coat. It doesn't belong

a on paying for our meal.
b for forgetting her name.
c about winning the prize.
d for the same train as you.
e to me.
f with them about the price.
g at the station.
h at me.

3 Complete the sentences with the correct preposition.

1 My grandmother is always complaining about the weather.
2 I dream ________ travelling round the world one day.
3 The man argued ________ the waiter about the bill.
4 They didn't listen ________ the warning.
5 I smiled ________ Sally but she didn't recognize me.
6 Do you agree ________ me about the best way to go?
7 I didn't answer because I'm concentrating ________ my homework.
8 Nobody ever laughs ________ my father's jokes.

Verbs of movement

4 Rewrite the sentences using the correct form of a word from the box.

dart hobble limp pace stride ~~stroll~~ tear trudge

1 The guests **were walking** in the gardens of the hotel **for pleasure**.
The guests were strolling in the gardens of the hotel.
2 The farmer **walked with a big effort** through the snow to feed the animals.
3 My father **walked** into the room **with long steps** and sat down at the head of the table.
4 Everybody **ran quickly** into their houses when they heard the explosion.
5 The old lady's feet were hurting, so she **walked** across the road **with difficulty**.
6 He **walked up and down** in the room, waiting for his son to come home.
7 She had sprained her ankle, so she **was walking with difficulty**.
8 The children **ran in a dangerous way** down the street to greet their father.

The passive

1 Choose the correct alternative, active or passive.

1 What language **is spoken** / **speaks** in Brazil?
2 Police **have arrested** / **have been arrested** two boys for shoplifting.
3 The council replaced the plants that **had been stolen** / **had stolen.**
4 A new school **has built** / **has been built** near my house.
5 The first World Cup **plays** / **was played** in 1930.
6 We **ride** / **are ridden** our mountain bikes at the weekend.
7 Levi Strauss **made** / **was made** the first pair of jeans.
8 The meeting **will hold** / **will be held** next Monday.

2 Complete the sentences using the passive form of the verb in brackets.

1 Paper was invented by the Chinese 2,000 years ago. (invent)
2 Today mobile phones ________ in many different countries. (make)
3 Kay's happy because she ________ a pay rise. (give)
4 Those trees ________ next week to make room for a housing estate. (cut down)
5 They were late because the flight ________. (delay)
6 George couldn't find his wallet because it ________. (steal)
7 Reality shows ________ by millions of people every week. (watch)
8 Classes ________ next Thursday because of the general election. (cancel)

3 Use the words to make passive sentences. Use *by* where necessary.

1 *Stuart Little* / read / children all over the world.
Stuart Little is read by children all over the world.
2 UNICEF / sponsor / the Barcelona football team.
____
3 The prize / give / the head teacher tomorrow.
____
4 *The Da Vinci Code* / write / Dan Brown.
____
5 We couldn't drive because our car / damage / vandals.
____
6 Because of the accident this morning the motorway / close / police.
____

4 Complete the article about the footballer Pelé with the passive form of the verbs in brackets.

Edison Arantes do Nascimiento [1] is known (know) as Pelé, the greatest footballer of all time. He [2] ________ (give) the nickname by his friends at school, but even now he has no idea what it means.

Pelé [3] ________ (teach) to play football by his father, and he joined his first professional team when he was 15. He soon became the top goal scorer in the league, and at the age of 17 he [4] ________ (ask) to join the national team. After the 1962 World Cup he [5] ________ (offer) massive fees by several European clubs, but the Brazilian government declared him an 'official national treasure' to prevent him from transferring out of the country.

Pelé played his last match on 1st October 1977 and since then he has been the official football ambassador for FIFA. He has published several autobiographies and a number of films [6] ________ (make) about his life.

CHALLENGE!

Find out about another sports person and write a short article. Include information about

- the sports person's education
- the sports person's achievements
- what they're doing now.

____
____
____
____
____
____

Getting from A to B

1 Label the photos.

carriage departures board information desk
railway track rucksack trolley

2 Write the following words in the columns. Words can go in more than one column.

air traffic controller cab carriage customs
~~departures board~~ escalator passport control
rucksack railway traffic jam track trolley

At an airport	At a train station	In the street
departures board	departures board	______
______	______	______
______	______	______
______	______	______
______	______	______
______	______	______
______	______	______
______	______	______
______	______	______
______	______	______

3 Complete the sentences and do the puzzle.

Across

2 You'd better not take the slow ______ train. It takes five hours to reach Manchester.

3 She said she couldn't afford to use public transport any more, as it's too ______.

5 The seats on the bus are so ______ that I prefer to stand.

6 I had to work a different shift last week, and was amazed how ______ it is to travel on public transport outside the rush hour.

Down

1 The streets are much more ______ for children than they used to be when there was less traffic.

2 I find waiting in queues for buses and trains quite ______, so I usually walk or cycle to work.

4 You can buy ______ train tickets if you book them far enough in advance.

CHALLENGE!

Write about the forms of transport in your country. Say which is the best / the worst, and give reasons.

______
______
______
______
______
______

Indefinite pronouns: *some-*, *any-*, *no-*

1 **Complete the sentences with *some/any* + *-body/-thing/-where*.**

1 We'd like something hot to drink.
2 I haven't got ___________ to wear to Chloë's house.
3 Can ___________ help me push my car, please?
4 Let's go on holiday ___________ near the sea.
5 Has ___________ seen my glasses?
6 She's so hungry, she'll eat ___________!

2 **Rewrite the *no* + *-body/-thing/-where* sentences with *any* + *-body/-thing/-where* and vice versa.**

1 We didn't go anywhere special last weekend.
We went nowhere special last weekend.
2 Don't shout at him! He's done nothing wrong!
____
3 Katie hasn't seen anybody today.
____
4 That train is going nowhere.
____
5 There was nobody at the airport to meet us.
____
6 I'm bored. I haven't got anything to do.
____

3 **Rewrite the sentences that are incorrect.**

1 We were tired but we didn't have nowhere to sleep.
We were tired but we didn't have anywhere to sleep.
2 Has somebody seen my passport?
____
3 There was nothing on the TV, so we turned it off.
____
4 Would you like something to eat?
____
5 There wasn't nobody at the check-in desk.
____
6 Can I have anything to drink?
____
7 I'll move anywhere, as long as it's out of the city centre.
____
8 He's hungry because he didn't have something for breakfast.
____

4 **Complete the article with *some/any/no* + *-body/-thing/-where*.**

Low-cost flights may mean you can go away [1] somewhere nice for the same price as it costs to stay at home, but there is another side to the story. Every time [2] ___________ takes a return flight from London to New York, they produce about 1.2 tonnes of carbon dioxide. You can't travel [3] ___________ by plane without contributing to global warming.

So, can [4] ___________ be done to solve the problem? Currently, governments seem to be doing next to [5] ___________ to control the carbon emissions from aircraft. [6] ___________ has managed to discover an alternative fuel to kerosene. The damage airlines do to society through climate change is not [7] ___________ that is easy to calculate in financial terms. And relying on individuals to limit the flights they take is also not the answer. There isn't [8] ___________ who would choose a train over a plane when they have to travel over 1,000 kilometres to a business meeting or a family wedding.

One thing is clear. If the issue of aircraft carbon emissions is not addressed properly, there will soon be [9] ___________ to fly to.

CHALLENGE!

Read the questions and use *some/any/no* + *-body/-thing/-where* to write a sentence.

Who would you like to be your best friend?
My best friend would be somebody who loves sports like I do, because we could play football together and go to matches.

What would you like for your next birthday?
____
____

Where would you like to go for your next holiday?
____
____

A postcard

Preparation

1 Match the two halves to make introductory 'it' sentences.

1 It's impossible d
2 It's a good job ___
3 It's a shame ___
4 It was really dangerous driving ___
5 It's been snowing ___
6 It's no ___
7 It took ___
8 It isn't worth ___

a use complaining.
b since we arrived.
c so long to get here.
d to go out.
e you're not here.
f we brought some warm clothes.
g hoping things will get better soon.
h on the motorway.

2 Read the postcard and write an 'it' phrase from exercise 1 in each space. There are two phrases that you do not need.

Dear Cath and Paul,
Weather is freezing, so 1 ______________.
Our room has no heating, so it's a bit chilly.
2 ______________. *Don't think we'll be using our swimming costumes, but* 3 ______________ *to the travel company because it's not their fault. Journey down was awful because of the bad weather.*
4 ______________. *We all got really bored in the car because* 5 ______________ *– more than five hours. Not sure what we'll do tomorrow because* 6 ______________.
Love
Dave and Alison

3 Look at the sentences for beginning and ending postcards. Write B for the beginnings and E for the endings.

1 Having an awful time in Finland and can't wait to go home. ___
2 We're off to the pool now. ___
3 Arrived in Rome last night and we're leaving again this morning. ___
4 I'd better post this now. ___
5 I'm on holiday in the Alps, but I wish I wasn't. ___
6 It's time for bed now. ___
7 We're in the south of France, and we hate it. ___
8 Must go now. I've run out of space again. ___

4 Match a word in Box A with a word in Box B to make holiday problems.

A	B
a disastrous chilly an unfinished disgusting	food weather journey hotel

A	B
a rocky unfriendly damp an incompetent	rooms airline beach people

Writing task

5 In your notebook write a postcard to your family about a trip abroad. Use the Writing Bank on page 91 to help you. Write 75–100 words and include the following information:

- some of the problems from exercise 4
- one or two problems of your own.

Check your work

Have you

☐ started and finished your postcard appropriately?
☐ used some phrases with 'it'?
☐ written 75–100 words?
☐ checked grammar, spelling and punctuation?

SELF CHECK 8: GRAMMAR

1 Make the sentences passive. Use by where necessary.

1 Levi Strauss made the first jeans.
The first jeans were made by Levi Strauss.

2 People speak Portuguese in Brazil.
Portuguese ______________________.

3 They'll probably cancel your flight because of the bad weather.
Your flight ______________________.

4 They've planted some beautiful flowers in my street.
Some beautiful flowers ______________________.

5 I thought you had sold your house.
I thought your house ______________________.

6 Alexander Graham Bell invented the telephone in 1876.
The telephone ______________________.

7 People wear kimonos in Japan.
Kimonos ______________________.

8 Scientists have developed a new treatment for malaria.
A new treatment for malaria ______________________.

9 They had bought too much food for the picnic.
Too much food ______________________.

10 The waitress will take your order.
Your order ______________________.

Your score /10

2 Complete the sentences with the correct passive form of the verbs in brackets.

1 The new Mini __________ in Cowley, Oxford. (make)

2 The bank robbers __________ until they tried to leave the country. (not arrest)

3 The police could not work out how the paintings __________. (steal)

4 Our school looks much better. All the classrooms __________ recently. (paint)

5 Last Saturday's match __________ by the local team. (win)

6 Uniforms __________ in many schools in Britain nowadays. (not wear)

7 A new station __________ near my house so I've started taking the train to work. (build)

8 The meeting __________ until next week. (hold)

9 So much __________ already __________ about this man that it's impossible to add anything new. (write)

10 The bridge __________ in time for next summer. (not finish)

Your score /10

3 Complete the sentences with an indefinite pronoun.

1 It was a waste of time cooking because __________ was hungry.

2 I want to go __________ hot for my holidays.

3 Would you like __________ to drink?

4 There won't be __________ home if you call now.

5 I didn't buy the picture because I have __________ to put it.

6 Did you get __________ nice in the sales?

7 I need __________ to look after my dog for the weekend.

8 We're going shopping because there's __________ in the fridge.

9 I can't find my wallet __________.

10 I want to go __________ nice and warm for my next holiday.

Your score /10

4 Complete the dialogues with an indefinite pronoun.

1 A What are you doing tonight?
B __________ special. I don't have any plans.

2 A Where does Jack live?
B __________ near the airport.

3 A Where are you going on holiday?
B __________. We're staying at home this year.

4 A What shall we cook for dinner?
B __________. I really don't mind.

5 A Who went to Sam's house?
B __________ I knew. They were all friends of his brother.

6 A What are you going to buy?
B __________ for my sister's birthday.

7 A What are you doing here?
B I'm waiting for __________.

8 A Why didn't you enjoy the party?
B Because I didn't know __________.

9 A Where shall we go at the weekend?
B __________. It really doesn't matter.

10 A Who was that you were talking to?
B __________ from my class.

Your score /10

Total /40

SELF CHECK 8: VOCABULARY

1 Complete the vocabulary quiz with words from Unit 8.

Quiz

1 _________ animals are active at night.

2 I had to stay in hospital for six months with a broken leg. Now I always _________ when I walk and I can't run very well.

3 Wild cats have beautiful _________ on their coats.

4 You need to be _________ to track wild animals, so that they don't hear you approaching.

5 He's always boasting _________ his family connections.

6 The sight of the eagle in full flight was simply _________.

7 I'm sorry, but I don't agree _________ you.

8 I find it more _________ to travel by train because I don't have to concentrate on driving.

9 It rained heavily during the walk, and we all _________ home through the thick mud.

10 There are no audio announcements in the airport, so you need to keep an eye on the _________.

11 My heart started _________ when I heard a noise in the living room.

12 I've always dreamed _________ going to Australia.

13 We needed a _________ to carry all our bags.

14 It was a beautiful day, so they _________ through the country enjoying the sun.

15 I was _________ with my brother for breaking my MP4 player.

16 I have a phobia about lifts, so I always use the _________.

17 We were late for work, so we decided to take a _________.

18 The player with the injured ankle _________ off the pitch.

19 We forgot to take an umbrella and so we got _________.

20 We can't begin to combat pollution without finding forms of transport that are more _________.

Your score ___ /20

2 Complete the text with the correct words, (a–d).

A cat called Jasper became famous for getting on the same bus every day and going for a ride around town. He certainly chose the right form of transport. It was [1] _________, because he didn't have to pay, [2] _________, because he always knew what time the bus was coming, and [3] _________, because he always got his favourite seat and curled up on it for a sleep. Jasper would [4] _________ at the bus stop at the same time every day and sit waiting patiently for the bus to come. When it came [5] _________ round the corner, Jasper would stand up and [6] _________ over to the kerb before [7] _________ on board. The passengers all found it amusing, and nobody [8] _________ about the cat getting a free ride; in fact, they made sure that he got off at the right stop. Jasper's owner knew nothing about this, and assumed that, as a [9] _________ creature, Jasper was at home asleep all day. 'At least if he's on a bus, I know he's [10] _________,' she laughed.

1 **a** limp **b** relaxing **c** slow **d** cheap
2 **a** reliable **b** stealthy **c** awesome **d** environmentally-friendly
3 **a** nocturnal **b** safe **c** awesome **d** comfortable
4 **a** dream **b** tear **c** pace **d** arrive
5 **a** darting **b** trundling **c** hobbling **d** trudging
6 **a** arrive **b** listen **c** stroll **d** limp
7 **a** springing **b** markings **c** trundling **d** boasting
8 **a** soaked **b** strolled **c** complained **d** hurtled
9 **a** dangerous **b** nocturnal **c** stressful **d** inconvenient
10 **a** safe **b** slow **c** reliable **d** cheap

Your score ___ /10

Total ___ /30

9 Spend, spend, spend!

READING

Before reading: Giving away

1 Write the numbers and dates in words.

1 1995 nineteen ninety five
2 20,359 ____
3 45,000,000 ____
4 2005 ____
5 36,400 ____
6 2010 ____

2 Read the text and match the headings (1–6) with the paragraphs (A–E). There is one heading that you do not need.

1 Who got the money?
2 What's next?
3 What did he do?
4 What went wrong?
5 What's the task?
6 What was their excuse?

3 Match the two halves of the sentences.

1 Ben Way gave a volunteer some money so that ____
2 Contestants have to promise to give some money away in order to ____
3 The millionaires were sent to poor areas to ____
4 Ufu Niazi had been working with no pay to ____
5 Ben gave some money to the Pedro Club so that ____
6 The television crew accompanied Ben in order to ____

a get on the show.
b ensure the centre stayed open.
c he could get married.
d film the documentary.
e find deserving causes for their money.
f it would be easier to run.

Secret Millionaire

***Secret Millionaire* is a reality show with a difference. Instead of winning fantastic cash prizes, contestants have to pay as much as £50,000 each to take part.**

A ____

The contestants of the first series were five millionaires of different ages and from different walks of life. They were taken out of their comfortable carefree environments and sent to some of the poorest parts of Britain. Here they had to integrate into the community and live on the minimum wage for ten days. At the end of the programme, they decided which of the people they met deserved their money most.

B ____

The first contestant was 26-year-old Ben Way, who is reputedly worth around £25 million. Ben's destination was the London district of Hackney, commonly known as the 'gun mile'. His explanation for the television crew following him everywhere was that they were filming a documentary about how poor people from the countryside mixed with poor people from the city.

C ____

Ben spent an eye-opening ten days working at the Pedro Club, a youth centre for disadvantaged youngsters. Run by manager Ufu Niazi, the centre was financed purely by donations and grants, and Ufu had been working with no pay for over two years.

D ____

At the end of the show Ben gave £20,000 to the Pedro Club for renovation, wages, and to build a recording studio on the premises, which could be rented out to provide a permanent source of income for the centre. Ben also gave money to one of the volunteers so that he could get married, and to one of the members to realize his dream of becoming a fashion designer.

E ____

The series portrayed millionaires as real people who seemed quite happy to give away part of their fortune. We can only hope that *Secret Millionaire* continues well into the future so that even more cash is made available to deserving causes.

VOCABULARY

Thanks a million

1 Replace the words in bold with a synonym.

1 Sandra's main **objective** in life is to be happy. goal
2 The new restaurant on the High Street is **becoming successful** very quickly. ______
3 The new TV show will be **presented** by a famous musician. ______
4 The 90-year-old artist **died** peacefully in his sleep. ______
5 My grandmother has no **sad feelings** about her life. ______
6 Van Gogh's *Sunflowers* reached a record price in the **public sale** last week. ______
7 It seems like the **whole** school has heard about my embarrassing moment yesterday. ______
8 My cousin has decided to **go and live permanently** in Australia. ______
9 My brother has a **natural skill** for maths. ______
10 My father is thinking of setting up a new **project** importing and exporting old cars. ______
11 Tom waited until after lunch to open the **presents** his guests had brought. ______
12 A wealthy **businessman** is going to run the first flights for tourists into space. ______
13 When she died, she **gave** all her money to the local children's home. ______
14 My best friend has a **very big** collection of CDs. ______
15 I thought I would pass easily. **The opposite was true and** I failed with a very low mark. ______

Inseparable phrasal verbs

2 Match the two parts of the sentences.

1 Those shoes really don't go — h
2 While we were away, a burglar broke
3 When I need money, I can always count
4 While we were tidying the attic, we came
5 I told my sister that I would look
6 My brother always picks
7 After we'd finished the exam we went
8 She's always falling out

a over the answers with our teacher.
b after her baby while she was out.
c with her sister.
d on me when my parents aren't looking.
e across a valuable painting.
f on my father.
g into our house.
h with that coat.

3 Complete the sentences with the correct form of the phrasal verb in brackets and an object from the box.

me   some old photos   ~~the dress~~   the explanation   the party   the school   us   you

1 I need a coat to go with the dress I've bought for the wedding. (go with)
2 Some students ______ last night to steal the exam papers. (break into)
3 Can I ______ to help me organize Dad's 50th birthday party? (count on)
4 Harry ______ next weekend. (look forward to)
5 They ______ while they were tidying the cupboard. (come across)
6 My big sister used to ______ when I was little. (pick on)
7 Our grandparents ______ when our parents had to go to work. (look after)
8 The teacher ______ again, but we still didn't understand. (go over)

Verb phrases: money

4 Complete the sentences with the correct form of a verb from the box.

ask for   invest   ~~pay~~   save up   spend   take

1 We paid for our last holiday by credit card.
2 My sister ______ too much money on clothes.
3 Duncan lost all the money he ______ in his brother's company.
4 I'm not going out this term because I ______ for a motorbike.
5 Jade ______ €100 out of the cash machine last night.
6 They ______ a loan because they wanted to buy a new car.

GRAMMAR

have something done

1 Put the words in order to make sentences or questions.

1 my photo / going to / have / tomorrow / I'm / taken
I'm going to have my photo taken tomorrow.
2 cut / Jessica / her hair / is having
______
3 had / Georgia / painted / last week / her nails
______
4 had / stolen / his mobile phone / Leo / has
______
5 yesterday / you / tested / Did / have / your eyes
______?
6 you / your teeth / Have / whitened / had
______?

2 Complete the sentence with the correct form of *have something done* and the words in brackets.

1 Marcus isn't cleaning his house. (cleaned)
He's having his house cleaned.
2 I didn't repair my car. (repaired)
I ______
3 Evan isn't going to test his eyes. (tested)
He ______
4 Ruby hasn't dyed her hair. (dyed)
She ______
5 Gary isn't going to cut his hair. (cut)
He ______
6 We aren't decorating our house. (decorated)
We ______
7 They don't iron their clothes. (ironed)
They ______

3 Complete the dialogues with the correct reflexive pronoun.

1 Did she have her car repaired?
No, she repaired it herself.
2 Does he have his shirts ironed?
No, he irons them ______.
3 Did you have your make-up done professionally?
No, I did it ______.
4 Are we going to have the house painted?
No, we're going to paint it ______.
5 Are they going to have the dresses made?
No, they're going to make them ______.
6 Am I having my room tidied tomorrow?
No, you're doing it ______.
7 Did you have that wall built?
No, I built it ______.

4 Complete the sentences with the correct form of the verbs. One sentence in each pair needs a reflexive pronoun.

1 cut
a Erin cut her finger while she was peeling carrots.
b Steve ______ while he was shaving.

2 enjoy
a Did you ______ the meal?
b Did you ______ at the theatre?

3 control
a Evie can't ______ when she gets angry.
b Mr Harris can't ______ the class on Friday afternoons.

4 hurt
a My brother ______ his leg playing football.
b My sister ______ playing in the park.

5 taught
a Millie ______ to speak Italian.
b Thomas ______ his brother to read.

6 look after
a The children are old enough to ______.
b Some friends ______ the children when their mother is at work.

CHALLENGE!

Look at the following chores. Does someone do them for you, or do you do them yourself? Write sentences using *have something done* or a reflexive pronoun.

- make your bed
- pack your school bag
- clean your room
- buy your clothes
- pay for your phone calls

______
______
______
______
______
______

Money and finance

1 Match the words (1–12) with the words in the box to make expressions about money and finance.

account account card card change currency debt interest ~~machine~~ money number rate

1 cash machine
2 credit ______
3 in ______
4 pocket ______
5 exchange ______
6 rate of ______
7 current ______
8 savings ______
9 debit ______
10 PIN ______
11 foreign ______
12 small ______

2 Complete sentences (1–12) with expressions from exercise 1.

1 You pay by credit card when you don't want the money to leave your account the same day.
2 When you go abroad, it's a good idea to take some ______ with you.
3 You often need some ______ to buy a coffee from a drinks machine.
4 If you don't know your ______, you can't use your card.
5 Most people take money out of a ______ now, instead of queuing up in the bank.
6 People put the money they don't want to spend into a ______.
7 Paying by ______ means the money is taken from your account the same day.
8 You are ______ if you are paying off a loan.
9 A small amount of money given by parents to their children on a weekly basis is called ______.
10 The ______ tells you how much your currency is worth in dollars or pounds, for example.
11 The ______ is the percentage that a bank charges you on a loan you are paying back.
12 A person's ______ is the account they use for day-to-day expenses.

3 Choose the correct alternatives.

1 Joe **owes** / **affords** me £25 for his concert ticket.
2 I **lent** / **borrowed** Sean some money last week, but he still hasn't given it back.
3 The new supermarket **costs** / **charges** 5p for plastic bags.
4 Josh needs some money, so he's going to **buy** / **sell** his motorbike.
5 Olivia **wastes** / **pays** her pocket money on CDs she never listens to.
6 The jacket I bought is too small, so I'm going to **take** / **bring** it back to the shop.
7 We can't **afford** / **pay** a new car, so we're getting a second-hand one.
8 Bethany **spends** / **buys** a lot of money on clothes.

4 Match the two halves of the sentences.

1 I borrowed £50 h
2 How much do you spend ___
3 John refused to pay ___
4 The taxi driver charged us an extra £5 ___
5 We bought our car ___
6 Jasmine's saving up ___
7 Patrick pays £10 ___
8 Carol will sell her leather jacket ___

a for her gap year trip.
b from our neighbour.
c for his meal because it was so disgusting.
d to the person who offers her the most money.
e for each suitcase we had.
f on computer games?
g into his savings account every month.
h from my brother. He's very kind.

CHALLENGE!

Have you ever had a bad experience with money? Explain what happened.

Third conditional

1 Match two halves of the sentences to make third conditional sentences.

1 If we'd saved some money, c
2 If you hadn't waited until the sales, ___
3 If she hadn't had the receipt, ___
4 She would have had a coffee ___
5 I would have been able to get some money out ___
6 Hayden wouldn't have lent him the money ___

a if she'd had any small change for the machine.
b if he'd known he wasn't going to give it back.
c we would have been able to afford a new car.
d if I hadn't forgotten my PIN number.
e you would have paid more for your skirt.
f she wouldn't have got a refund on the trousers.

2 Use the words to make third conditional sentences. Remember to use a comma (,) where necessary.

1 If / Jason / not spend / all his pocket money / he / be able to / afford / a new MP3 player.
If Jason hadn't spent all his pocket money, he'd be able to afford a new MP3 player.
2 If / we / go / to the right gate / we / not miss / the flight.
___
3 If / they / not leave / home earlier / they / get stuck / in a traffic jam.
___
4 They / run out / of petrol / if / they / not stop / at the last petrol station.
___
5 He / break / his leg / if / he / fell off / the stepladder.
___
6 They / not fall out / if / he not forgot / Ellie's birthday.
___

3 Rewrite the *'d* phrases with *had* or *would*.

1 If I'd taken some money out ...
If I had taken some money out ...
2 I'd have bought the laptop if ...
___
3 They'd have borrowed the money if ...
___
4 ... if they'd known ...
___
5 They'd have given us a discount if ...
___
6 ... if it'd been in the sale ...
___

4 Read Alan's regrets and complete the sentences.

I didn't study much at school, so I didn't pass my exams. I found it difficult to find a job because I didn't have any qualifications. I worked as a labourer until I hurt my back. I lived with my mother because I didn't earn enough money. I didn't meet many friends because I couldn't go out. I got married very late so I didn't have any children. I never went abroad because I was always broke. I've had a hard life.

1 If he'd studied more at school, he'd have passed his exams.
2 If ___ some qualifications, he ___ a job more easily.
3 If ___ as a labourer, he ___ his back.
4 He ___ with his mother if ___ more money.
5 He ___ more friends if ___ to go out.
6 If ___ earlier, he ___ children.
7 He ___ abroad if ___ broke.

CHALLENGE!

Have you got any regrets about your life? Write about them here, using the third conditional.

___

WRITING

A formal letter: asking for information

Preparation

1 **Read the formal letter asking for information and complete it with the indirect questions (A–C).**

A please can you tell me if this would be possible
B could you tell me how many passengers your minivans carry
C would you mind telling me when we will have to reserve the minivan

Dear Sir or Madam,
I recently saw your advertisement for the rental of minivans in Driving Holidays magazine, and I have a few queries.
I am planning a driving holiday through Spain and France this summer with six friends. [1] ______, and which model would be the most suitable for our group?
We are planning our trip for the month of August, so [2] ______ to make sure there is a van available for us? Would you also mind confirming that the minivans are fully equipped with air conditioning?
We are considering driving the minivan down to the South of Spain and then flying back to Britain. [3] ______, and how much the rental would increase if we dropped the minivan off in Seville?
Finally, would you mind telling me if you have a minimum age limit for renting your minivans?

I look forward to hearing from you.
Yours faithfully,

Sarah Coombs

Sarah Coombs

2 **Look at the letter and find formal equivalents for the informal phrases.**

INFORMAL	FORMAL
I've got some questions	1 *I have a few queries*
which would be the best model	2 ______
to make sure there is a van for us	3 ______
how much the rental would go up	4 ______
Please write soon	5 ______
Best wishes	6 ______

3 **Number the features in the order in which they appear in the letter.**

___ Signature
___ Sentence requesting a reply
___ Reason for writing
___ Main query
___ Name
1 Greeting
___ Third query
___ Final query
___ Second query
___ Sign-off

Writing task

4 **In your notebook write a formal letter asking for information about the apartments advertised below. Use the Writing Bank on page 91 to help you. Write 150–200 words and include the following:**

- your reason for writing
- indirect questions to ask for information.

Check your work

Have you

☐ organized your queries into paragraphs?
☐ written 150–200 words?
☐ checked grammar, spelling and punctuation?

SELF CHECK 9: GRAMMAR

1 Rewrite the sentences using *have something done*.

1 Somebody is painting their house.
They're ______________________.

2 Somebody has repaired my bike.
I ______________________.

3 Nobody installed a new shower for him.
He ______________________.

4 Somebody is going to cut my sister's hair.
My sister ______________________.

5 Is somebody examining Jamie's arm?
Is Jamie ______________________?

6 Nobody has tested my eyes for a long time.
I ______________________.

7 Somebody cleaned our carpet last week.
We ______________________.

8 Is somebody going to take your photo?
Are you ______________________?

Your score ___ **/8**

2 Complete the dialogues with the correct reflexive pronouns.

1 A Did your Dad give you the money for your car?
B No, I saved up for it ________.

2 A Can you iron our uniforms for us, please?
B No, I'm busy. You can do it ________.

3 A Did your sister have her motorbike repaired?
B No, she didn't. She repaired it ________.

4 A Do you have to help your little brother get dressed?
B No, I don't. He dresses ________.

5 A Did your parents help you pay for your flat?
B No, we paid for it ________.

6 A Can you help me with my homework?
B No, I'm going out. You can do it ________.

7 A How do I turn off the camera?
B It turns off ________ when it isn't being used.

8 A Did they have their house decorated?
B No, they decorated it ________.

Your score ___ **/8**

3 Complete the third conditional sentences with the correct form of the verbs in brackets. Use short forms.

1 If I ____________ in the sun, ____________ sunburnt. (not sit / not get)

2 I ____________ to work if I ____________ about the accident. (not drive / know)

3 If he ____________ late, he ____________ his train. (not be / not miss)

4 If you ____________ to school today, what ____________ you ____________? (not come / do)

5 We ____________ you some money if you ____________ us. (lend / ask)

6 She ____________ the burglar if she ____________ her keys. (not see / not forget)

7 ____________ you ____________ my birthday if I ____________ you? (remember / not remind)

8 If I ____________ off my bike, I ____________ my leg. (not fall / not break)

Your score ___ **/16**

4 Rewrite the sentences as third conditional sentences.

1 He didn't have enough money. He didn't buy the laptop.
______________________________.

2 She spoke good English. They offered her a job.
______________________________.

3 We got lost. We didn't take a map.
______________________________.

4 Their best player was injured. They didn't win the match.
______________________________.

5 I broke my glasses. I dropped them.
______________________________.

6 You lost your camera. You left it on the bus.
______________________________.

7 He had a very big lunch. He feels tired now.
______________________________.

8 You didn't take your umbrella. You got wet.
______________________________.

Your score ___ **/8**

Total ___ **/40**

SELF CHECK 9: VOCABULARY

1 Complete the vocabulary quiz with words from Unit 9.

Quiz

1 An _________ is a person who risks his money on a new idea.

2 It isn't really important to buy a handbag that _________ your shoes these days.

3 Janet has a _________ for music. She plays the piano, the violin and the trumpet.

4 After a holiday in Canada, my family decided to _________ there permanently.

5 We're going to _________ all our old books and toys to charity.

6 We'll need some foreign _________ for our trip to the States.

7 They bought some second-hand furniture at an _________, but they spent more than they'd intended to.

8 Some children don't get much _________ from their parents, so they often get a part-time job.

9 We paid our hotel bill by _________.

10 I couldn't get hold of any money because the _________ at the station was out of order.

11 Somebody _________ into their house while they were away.

12 Laura came _________ some old family photos from her grandmother while she was cleaning out her mother's room.

13 I'm _________ on all my friends to come to my birthday party.

14 My son came home crying one day, saying that the other children had _________ him.

15 When you buy something, you should always ask for a _________.

16 When I launched my online shop, things were fairly quiet for the first six months. But then business _________.

17 If I won £1 million, I'd spend some of it and _________ the rest.

18 He had _________ for ages to buy his new guitar, so he was heartbroken when it got stolen.

19 Many shops and businesses ask for your _________ rather than your signature when paying for goods by card.

20 In some shops, you have to pay in cash or by card, as they no long accept _________.

Your score /20

2 Complete the text with suitable verbs.

Taking better care of your cash

Security

When you [1]_________ cash out of a cash machine, cover the keyboard when you [2]_________ in your PIN number. Somebody may be watching.

When you [3]_________ by credit card in a restaurant, don't let staff take your card away. Somebody may copy it.

When you purchase goods on the internet, never [4]_________ a debit card. Somebody may access your computer and use your identity.

When you are in a crowd, [5]_________ after your wallet carefully. Somebody may have the opportunity to steal it.

If a burglar [6]_________ into your house and takes your bank cards, cancel them immediately. They may try to use them.

Borrowing

When you need a small amount of money, you can usually [7]_________ on a friend to lend it to you. Always pay them back quickly.

When you need a larger amount, you can sometimes [8]_________ money from your family. Make it clear that the money is a loan, not a gift.

When you need a lot of money, you can go to a bank to [9]_________ for a loan. Make sure you choose your bank wisely.

When you accept a loan from a company, [10]_________ over the agreement carefully before you sign it. Consult an expert, if necessary.

Your score /10

Total /30

10 Inspiration

READING

Before reading: Art

1 **Join words in box A and box B to make compound nouns. Then complete the sentences.**

A	B
street	sculpture
oil	gallery
art	art
public	painting
living	place

1 The artist's work is displayed in a local art gallery.
2 A work which contains a real person is called a ________.
3 If it rains during an exhibition of ________, many of the exhibits get washed away.
4 Graffiti is always displayed in a ________.
5 Our friends have an ________ hanging in the living room.

2 **Read the text and choose the best answer.**

1 Wyland paints his pictures of whales
  a on the outside of buildings.
  b on the inside of buildings.
  c in art galleries.
  d in buildings by the sea.
2 Wyland's interest in whales started
  a when he saw one in a documentary.
  b when he started studying marine biology.
  c when he went to Canada.
  d when he was a teenager .
3 Wyland's murals are planned
  a carefully before he starts painting
  b when he's standing in front of the wall.
  c in a sketch he makes beforehand.
  d on his computer.
4 The main reason why Wyland paints whales is because
  a he likes them.
  b he wants to show people how beautiful they are.
  c he wants to save them from extinction.
  d they are very big.

Wyland's whales

Some of the largest and most beautiful outdoor murals in the world have been created by the American artist Robert Wyland, or 'Wyland' as he prefers to be called.

Wyland's murals depict an animal that he is passionate about: the whale. His inspiration lies in the whales he has studied and swum with as a diver and practising environmentalist.

Wyland's first encounter with the sea was on a family visit to California when he was 14. The experience of seeing his first whale in the Pacific Ocean had an enormous impact on his life and his future. When he returned home he threw himself into the study of marine life and started excelling in sport. In 1977 he painted his first whale mural in Laguna Beach, California, which is now a famous landmark. His goal is to paint 100 murals before 2011.

The whales in Wyland's murals are all painted life-size, which means they are absolutely huge. He never knows exactly what he is going to paint until he approaches the blank wall with his paint sprayer. His painting technique is also unusual, as he uses none of the traditional methods typical of such large projects, like sketches, outlines or grids. Most of his murals take about a week to make and he has done painting tours where he has painted 17 murals in 17 weeks.

However, Wyland does not only paint whales because he likes them. His main objective is to bring the plight of the whale to the attention of the public in the hope that they will not become extinct. And he has chosen his medium well. It is not easy to walk past one of his giant murals without admiring the beauty of his whales. We can only hope the real thing outlives Wyland's artistic representations of them.

Banksy and Pavement Picasso

1 Complete the sentences with the words in the box.

billboards brickwork charities claim depicting elaborate factors incorporates portable portraits potholes ~~primitive~~ publicity stunt striking swerve

1 Our campsite was quite primitive ________ as there was no running water.
2 Some of the ________ in these Victorian buildings is very ornate.
3 We had to park on the corner as the road was full of ________.
4 Kate wore a ________ dress to the dinner. She looked great!
5 This design ________ several themes that are very important to me.
6 We bought a picture ________ a garden scene for the wall of our living room.
7 He lived in a tree for a year as a ________ in order to draw attention to the loss of trees in our urban environment.
8 There are ________ advertising the new supermarket along the side of the motorway.
9 Technology has made everything so small now, whereas many years ago, not even a calculator was easily ________.
10 After the earthquake, many ________ went to the area to help the people affected.
11 When she fell down some stairs while wearing high heels, she tried to ________ that the Council was responsible.
12 Not all the people painting ________ in the square were very good. Mine didn't look anything like me.
13 One of the reasons for the increase in obesity is the availability of fast food, but there are other ________.
14 She invented an ________ story to explain to the teacher why she hadn't done her homework.
15 A boy ran out in front of my car, but I managed to ________ to avoid him.

Visual and performing arts

2 Complete the sentences.

1 A person who writes poetry is a poet ________.
2 A person who composes music is a ________.
3 A person who writes screenplays for films is a ________.
4 A person who plays a musical instrument is a ________.
5 A person who plays a role in a film is an ________.
6 A person who writes plays is a ________.
7 A person who creates sculptures is a ________.
8 A person who writes songs is a ________.

Idioms: art

3 Match the two parts of the sentences.

1 My mother's got organizing dinner parties d
2 My little cousin always steals ____
3 We have to face ____
4 They always make a song ____
5 I was late so I asked them to put ____
6 My parents can read me ____
7 When he found out the price he changed ____
8 He's very successful, but he's always ____

a the show at family parties.
b his tune about the trip.
c like a book.
d down to a fine art.
e blowing his own trumpet.
f me in the picture about the arrangements.
g the music over our mistake.
h and dance when they have to help.

4 Complete the sentences with an art idiom from exercise 3.

1 I always know what my sister's thinking. I can read her like a book.
2 He boasts a lot about being top of the class. He's always ________ ________ ________ ________.
3 The youngest actress got all the attention after the school play. She ________ ________ ________.
4 My mother only takes half an hour to prepare a fantastic meal. She's got cooking ________ ________ ________ ________ ________.
5 Since he visited London, my brother's decided he'd like to live there. He's ________ ________ ________ about moving abroad.
6 I missed the last drama class, so I didn't know who was going to be in the play. My friends soon ________ ________ ________ ________ ________.
7 My brother didn't stop complaining when I asked him to take me to the station. He made a complete ________ ________ ________ about it.
8 Alan has failed all his exams and now he has to tell his parents. He's going home to ________ ________ ________.

Participle clauses

1 **Choose the correct alternative, a present or past participle.**

1 The photos **taking** / **taken** at the school show haven't come out.
2 The sound technician is backstage **tested** / **testing** the mikes.
3 The money **collecting** / **collected** by the buskers will be donated to charity.
4 The gig **held** / **holding** last night was a complete success.
5 The model often **painting** / **painted** by Salvador Dalí was his wife, Gala.
6 The instrument **played** / **playing** by the lead violinist was a Stradivarius.
7 The audience **watching** / **watched** the play were completely absorbed in the plot.
8 We received a letter **inviting** / **invited** us to the opening night of the musical.

2 **Look at the picture and complete the sentences with the present participle or the past participle. Tick (✓) the information you think has been invented.**

1 The man wearing (wear) a white coat is taking something out of a basket.
2 The little girl ________ (look) at the basket is holding her big sister's hand.
3 The man ________ (sell) fruit and vegetables has sold lots of produce today.
4 The bird ________ (buy) by the man in the black jumper will be cooked for dinner.
5 The woman ________ (carry) the umbrella thinks that it's going to rain.
6 The vegetables ________ (not sell) in the market today will be kept until tomorrow.

3 **Rewrite the relative clauses as participle phrases.**

1 He played a trombone which belonged to his father.
He played a trombone belonging to his father.
2 On stage there's a woman who is brushing her hair.
____
3 She said thank you for the flowers which were given by the audience.
____
4 The scenery which was broken yesterday needs to be repaired.
____
5 The play which was performed by the National Theatre was an absolute disaster.
____
6 The guitarist who is playing in the gig isn't usually a member of the band.
____

CHALLENGE!

Invent some information about the people in the picture. Look at the questions to help you. Write the information as participle clauses.

What are the people wearing / doing?
Where are they going?
Why?

Art and artists

1 **Re-order the letters to make words related to the performance arts, then write them in the chart. Then write two more things that you can find in each place.**

~~riaa~~ bruskes stocmuse ragitiff glugnijg chartsore patrotri rieactl yenscer pginaitn tagse samluic lilts file

art gallery	theatre
1	4
2	5
3	6
	7
concert hall	**outside**
8 aria	11
9	12
10	13

2 **Match each word in the box with its definition.**

audience busker conductor juggler ~~model~~ soprano sound technician stage hand

1 a person who sits still for an artist to paint them model
2 a person who helps move the scenery ______
3 the person who leads an orchestra ______
4 a person who makes sure the mikes are working properly ______
5 the people watching the show ______
6 a person who plays music on the street ______
7 a person who performs on the street throwing and catching a set of balls ______
8 a woman who sings the highest notes in an aria ______

3 **Complete the story with the correct form of the verbs in the box.**

change into forget look move not work practise rehearse ~~test~~

The opening night was a complete disaster. The sound technician was late, so he didn't have time to [1] test the mikes. That meant we didn't realize they [2] ______ until after the play had started. The lead actor [3] ______ his opening lines, so the lead actress had to say them for him. But the lead actress hadn't had time to [4] ______ her costume, so she went though the entire first act with her jeans on. The stage hands wouldn't stop [5] ______ at the audience when they [6] ______ the scenery, so they kept on dropping all the props. And then in the interval one of the dancers twisted her ankle while she [7] ______ the steps. Honestly, I don't know why we spent so much time [8] ______!

CHALLENGE!

Write about an experience you or someone else has had on the stage or while performing.

Determiners: *all*, *each*, *every*, *few*, *little*, *no*

1 Rewrite the sentences that are incorrect.

1 Not much men enjoy stage musicals.
Not many men enjoy stage musicals.
2 Only a few people go on to sing opera.
3 Singers and dancers earn few money at first.
4 A lot of performers feel nervous when they start.
5 It doesn't take many time to feel more confident.
6 Little music students become famous.

2 Answer the questions using the words in brackets.

1 Did you see the series *The Choir*? (most)
I saw most of it.
2 Did you watch the Oscar ceremony on TV? (some)
I watched ________
3 Which sketches do you prefer? (any)
I don't like ________
4 Which scenery did you make? (all)
I made ________
5 How many English novels have you read? (a few)
I've read ________
6 Did you like the sculptures? (some)
I liked ________
7 Which James Bond films have you seen? (none)
I've seen ________

3 Use the words to make sentences. Remember to use 'of' where necessary.

1 Some / my friends / were at the opening night.
Some of my friends were at the opening night.
2 Most / the singers / came to the party after the show.
3 Few / people / knew about the exhibition.
4 Many / artists / have a second job.
5 All / these portraits / were painted by Rembrandt.
6 Most / people / prefer the cinema to the theatre.
7 The actress couldn't remember any / her lines.
8 Much / the scenery was made by the stage hands.

4 Choose the correct alternative.

1 The exhibition wasn't very popular. **Few** / **A few** people went to see it.
2 It's not the first time the lead singer has lost his voice. It's happened **few** / **a few** times before.
3 Van Gogh was nearly always broke. He made **a little** / **little** money from his work.
4 He had **little** / **a little** time so he took a break before finishing the picture.
5 The interview went well because the artist spoke **few** / **a few** words of English.
6 His room was quite bare because he had **a little** / **little** furniture.

CHALLENGE!

Look at the hobbies and write true sentences about you and your classmates.

Play in a band: Some of us play in a band.
Sing in a choir: ________
Go to gigs: ________
Visit art galleries: ________
Know how to juggle: ________
Do sketches: ________

An essay: giving your opinion

Preparation

1 **Match the photos to paragraphs (A–D).**

1 ________ 2 ________ 3 ________ 4 ________

A As a writer and artist, I'm often asked where my inspiration comes from. I have to say that if you have to look for inspiration, then you have no business being a writer. However, it is an interesting question to pursue.

B Speaking for myself, the inspiration for my work comes from many places. I've always been interested in history, all the amazing events that have happened over time. I love the way you can choose to inhabit a moment in time, in a particular country. And then of course, there's the fact that different people often have different perceptions of the same historical event.

C The second thing that fascinates me is family. What particularly interests me are the dynamics within a family group, how people get on with each other – or don't! I like exploring notions of kinship and family likeness, also the sharing of personality traits.

D I also love travelling – and I don't mean necessarily to far-flung exotic places. What intrigues me is seeing how humans have created and destroyed communities in social experiments or as a result of building trends.

E To sum up, the things that inspire me are those aspects of life that challenge us to think about our place in the world.

2 **Match the symbols and abbreviations with their meaning.**

1 ›	a and
2 comm^y	b because of
3 sth	c cause, lead to
4 =	d together
5 sb	e something
6 +	f or
7 cos of	g equals, is the same as
8 /	h somebody
9 tog	i community

3 **Add the abbreviations from exercise 2 to the plan for the essay in exercise 1. One of them is used twice.**

1 Intro – inspiration ¹______ all around ²______ you become artist ³______ writer

2 History – lots of events, places ⁴______ times to choose from
– people see history differently

3 Family – ⁵______ that forces people ⁶______
– not everyone is alike

4 Travelling – not just holidays – also local ⁷______
– where ⁸______ lives affects them ⁹______ isolation ¹⁰______ bad planning

5 Sum up – inspired by things that make us who we are

4 **Find three sentences in paragraphs B and C that can be turned into nominal subject clauses, and rewrite them using *what*.**

1 ______________________________

2 ______________________________

3 ______________________________

Writing task

5 **Choose an essay topic and write a brief essay plan, using notes where possible. Then write an essay of around 200 words. Use the Writing Bank on page 90 to help you.**

Check your work

Have you

- ☐ used notes in your essay plan?
- ☐ included an introduction and a conclusion?
- ☐ written around 200 words for your essay?
- ☐ checked grammar, spelling and punctuation in your essay?

SELF CHECK 10: GRAMMAR

1 Rewrite the sentences, using a present or past participle.

1 The boy who was waiting here has gone.

2 The woman who will accompany you will be here shortly.

3 All the places that were visited were ticked off.

4 The trams, which rattled through the streets all night, kept me awake.

5 The pages that have been marked are the ones you want to look at.

6 The animals that are usually seen here have moved to a different territory.

7 His brother, who was walking ten paces behind, looked miserable.

8 The sculptures, which were usually displayed in the main hall, were being cleaned.

9 This picture, which was taken when Bryony was only three, shows her dancing ability.

10 The film which will be shown here tomorrow will be the first in a series of Antonioni films.

Your score /10

2 Now replace the participle clause with a relative clause, using *which* or *who*.

1 The train, pulled by two engines, sped past the station.

2 We're going to see the new art gallery opening tomorrow.

3 The prisoner, escorted by two police officers, entered the courtroom.

4 I'm sure that the dinner, prepared by such an expert, will be very successful.

5 My office is in that block adjoining the business centre.

6 I've received two letters asking me for money I don't owe.

7 The two men, wearing overalls and trainers, climbed in through the window of the house.

8 These cottages, built in 1770, are under threat of demolition.

9 I was at school with that girl working behind the counter.

10 Anyone found in the changing rooms without good cause will be reported.

Your score /10

3 Choose the correct form.

1 We just had **a little** / **a few** rice and some chicken.
2 **All of** / **All** artists should be original thinkers.
3 The boys behaved themselves, except for **a few** / **a few of** the older ones.
4 It was terrible to think that, after all the hard work, **none** / **none of** it would count.
5 They've got **some** / **any** lovely apples and oranges.
6 **Much** / **Many** of his work is difficult to understand.
7 **Each of** / **Each** you should be proud of yourselves.
8 A lot of invitations were sent out, but in the end, **few** / **a few** people came.
9 **No** / **None** child will be allowed to go home early.
10 It's true that **most of the** / **most** people are honest.

Your score /10

4 Match the sentence halves.

1 Many of the
2 Each of
3 Every one
4 There was very little
5 Few
6 Much of the
7 I can't find any
8 I'd like to get
9 Every
10 Nothing

a of the soup left.
b some advice.
c of the guests turned up in the end, which was disappointing.
d people had never seen a ballet before.
e single plant is precious.
f my friends bought me a present.
g atmosphere was generated by anticipation.
h on this planet is responsible for preserving it.
i was done about the problem.
j maps of this town.

Your score /10

Total /40

SELF CHECK 10: VOCABULARY

1 Complete the vocabulary quiz with words from Unit 10.

Quiz

1 I think it must be easier to write the ________ to a song than to come up with a good melody.
2 A dog ran out in front of our car, so we had to ________ to avoid it.
3 The best way to advertise a new shopping mall is to put ________ on all the roads leading to it.
4 Our neighbour had hung a ________ new painting over the fireplace. We couldn't take our eyes off it!
5 The pattern on that dress is very ________. It's too detailed for my taste.
6 Anthony Hopkins played the ________ of Picasso in the film of the same name.
7 I don't like paintings of people. I find nature much more interesting, so I prefer ________.
8 After the fight, the two boys were called to the head teacher's office to ________ the music.
9 His parents made a ________ and dance about what he wore to the dinner.
10 I missed the argument, but my sister soon put me in the ________.
11 I don't usually give money to ________, but the girl playing the violin outside the supermarket was excellent.
12 There is a ________ of the King hanging in my father's office.
13 The ________ loved the show and everybody stood up and clapped at the end.
14 The original author of the novel agreed to write the ________ for the film.
15 My friends have just formed a band. They're playing their first ________ tomorrow night.
16 Everyone stared at the ________ painting on the gallery wall, but no one could agree what it was about.
17 She was very much against the idea at first, but she seems to have changed her ________.
18 My sister doesn't enjoy ________ as she doesn't like people bursting into song every five minutes.
19 I knew he'd change his mind about coming to the performance. I can read him like a ________.
20 The actors met up to read the ________ of the controversial new play.

Your score /20

2 Complete the text with the correct form of the words in brackets.

What's on?

Art

1 ________ (strike) paintings by one of the most prolific 2 ________ (art) of the twentieth century at the exhibition *Picasso: Challenging the Past*. The exhibition also includes some of the painter's lesser-known 3 ________ (sculpt). On at the National Gallery until June 7th.

Theatre

King Lear, written by the best-known of English 4 ________ (play), William Shakespeare. The portrayal of the last scene, in particular, is horribly believable. Atmosphere made realistic by superb 5 ________ (light) and music. Runs at the Arcola Theatre until March 14th.

Music

6 ________ (conduct) Christoph Eschenbach leads the 7 ________ (music) of the London Symphony Orchestra in their rendering of the German 8 ________ (compose) Johannes Brahms' Symphony No. 1. March 11th at the Royal Festival Hall.

Dance

A mixture of live 9 ________ (perform) and video suitable for 10 ________ (spectate) of any age. On at The Place in Duke's Road 13th and 14th March only.

Your score /10

Total /30

Before reading: Stereotypes

1 Choose the correct adjectives.

1 He's very **serious** / **funny**. He tells a lot of jokes.
2 She never says 'hello'. She's really **rude** / **polite**.
3 My aunt gives great presents. She's very **mean** / **generous**.
4 He doesn't say a lot. He's quite **quiet** / **talkative**.
5 She's never there when I need her. She's very **reliable** / **unreliable**.
6 My neighbours are always happy. They're very **cheerful** / **miserable**.
7 My brother's always sleeping. He's really **lazy** / **hard-working**.
8 He's always talking about himself. He's very **modest** / **arrogant**.

2 Read the text and match the nationalities with the adjectives.

1 German	a friendly
2 American	b kind
3 Finnish	c punctual

3 According to the text do the Germans, the Americans or the Finns show the following characteristics?

1 The ________ like their houses to look nice.
2 The ________ are very welcoming once they know you.
3 The ________ are proud of their country.
4 The ________ always do everything together.
5 The ________ are very punctual.
6 The ________ are extremely friendly.

CHALLENGE!

In your opinion, what are the main characteristics of the following?

The Japanese: ________ ________
The Germans: ________ ________
The Americans: ________ ________
The British: ________ ________
The Italians: ________ ________

British teenagers abroad

We all know what other nationalities say about the British! Now it's time for us to see how British teenagers get on abroad. We asked Mel, Becky and Ian for their views about the people they have met on their travels.

Mel, age 18, in Germany

I just can't believe how punctual the Germans are! Everything happens at exactly the time that they say it will, and if anything goes wrong, everybody gets really bad-tempered. In general, people can be a bit unfriendly if they don't know you, but once you've been introduced, they often invite you to their house for coffee and cakes.

Becky, age 19, in the USA

Americans find British people fascinating, so I spend hours talking to people. Everyone's really friendly, but sometimes it gets a bit much. My friends are really funny and we spend a lot of time at parties or at burger bars together. It's very difficult to do anything on your own because someone always wants to come with you!

Ian, age 17, in Finland

When I arrived here, the people I met, especially in shops and restaurants, seemed very serious. But my opinions changed when I made some friends. Finnish people, in fact, love having a good time and are very generous, too! In general, the people are patriotic and are keen to show you their country. They're also hard-working and extremely tidy at home!

ROUND-UP 3–4

Before reading: Healthy eating

1 **Match the words with their definitions.**

1 key
2 absence
3 consuming
4 control
5 preservatives
6 versions
7 devices
8 hidden
9 common
10 butter and milk

a varieties
b dairy products
c lack
d equipment
e usual
f eating
g significant
h monitor
i additives
j invisible

2 **Read the text and add the following phrases or clauses in the correct gap.**

A if families are no longer sitting down to eat together
B or two-for-one offers
C so that it didn't go off
D the extent of which is difficult to gauge in our diets

3 **Complete the sentences with words from the text.**

1 I always buy semi-skimmed milk. I never buy ________ milk.
2 We've got to have ________ in our diet. I couldn't eat the same thing all the time.
3 The fish in the market seems ________ than the fish in the shops.
4 I hate throwing out so much food. It's a terrible ________.
5 In Western countries, we all eat too much ________ food from tins and packets.
6 That ________ of rice is much too big. You don't need to eat that much.
7 I can't believe you think you're poor. You've no idea how ________ you are compared with many people.
8 It isn't enough to change your diet to become healthier. You also have to change your ________.

CHALLENGE!

Describe your favourite healthy meal.

____
____
____
____

Eating patterns: then and now

People often think that our diets were far worse sixty years ago because there were only full-fat versions of products like butter and milk. In those days, everyone was less aware of the need to eat healthily. There wasn't much variety, and the whole family ate at the same time.

However, people tended to be healthier then because there was no fast food. The food was fresher because preservatives didn't exist. Although this meant shopping for food every day [1]___, the result was less waste generally. It is easier to plan how much you'll need for one or two days' meals than for a whole week.

Besides preservatives, most processed food also contains largely hidden amounts of salt and fat, [2]___. Portion control has become significant, too. Because we are generally more affluent now, we have become used to having more of what we like whenever we want it. Shops are open seven days a week, sometimes up to 24 hours. Supermarkets offer ever-larger 'economy size' packets and cartons, [3]___. We have become very wasteful, while consuming more than ever.

Finally, technology has made us all less fit. Sixty years ago, fewer people had cars, and the absence of TV meant that children played outside. The labour-saving devices that we take so much for granted today were not so common then. For all its tedium, housework requires the same repetitive, stretching movements that many men and women pay to do at the gym. But one of the key changes in family life is our fractured lifestyle. No matter how healthy the food in the house, it is very difficult to control what people are eating [4]___.

Before reading: Mysteries

1 **Complete the summary of the Loch Ness Monster text on page 56 of the Students' Book with the words in the box.**

claim evidence fake genuine hoax

In 1934 an English surgeon called Wilson took a photo of a creature in Loch Ness and showed it as [1] ____________ that the Loch Ness Monster existed. The photo clearly showed an animal with a long neck and a small head, so people thought it might be [2] ____________. However, in 1993, a film director admitted that he had arranged the photo as a [3] ____________ to fool people into believing in Nessie. Ultimately it was proved that Wilson's photo was a [4] ____________, but there are still people who [5] ____________ that there is a monster in the lake.

2 **Read the text on crop circles. Are the sentences true or false?**

1. Chorley and Bower admitted they had created all the crop circles in southern England. ___
2. 'Cereology' is the study of crop circles. ___
3. 'Cereologists' believe most crop circles are unexplained. ___
4. Colin Andrews's theory is based on magnetism. ___
5. David Kingston doesn't believe in UFOs. ___
6. Kingston has proved that the crop circles make a strange sound. ___
7. The writer thinks people are fascinated by crop circles because the cause of crop circles is unknown. ___

CHALLENGE!

Find out about *Mary Celeste* – the greatest maritime mystery of all time. Write a brief summary of what happened.

____

____

____

____

Crop circles
– genuine or a hoax?

The patterns shown in the photograph are known as 'crop circles' and they caused great media speculation in the 1980s in Britain.

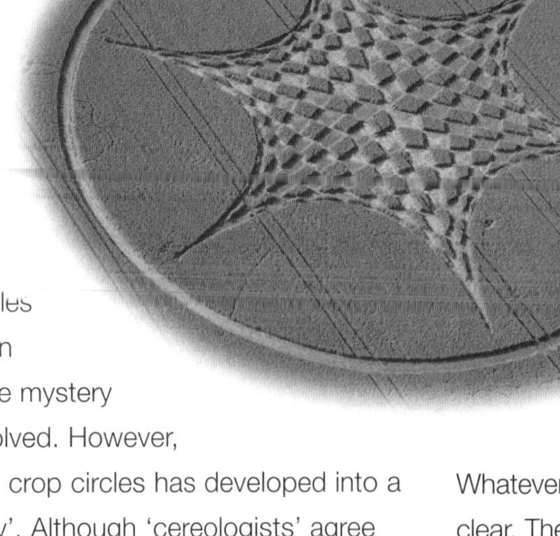

When two men, David Chorley and Douglas Bower, admitted in 1991 that they were responsible for more than 250 of the crop circles that appeared in southern England in the 1980s, the mystery seemed to have been solved. However, since then, research into crop circles has developed into a science called 'cereology'. Although 'cereologists' agree that about 80% of crop circles are man-made, they claim that another 20% remain unexplained.

So what causes the genuine crop circles? There are a number of possible explanations, some more credible than others. Colin Andrews has been researching crop circles since the 1980s. He claims they appear in fields in the summer because of a change in the Earth's magnetic field.

David Kingston, a leading UFO and crop circle researcher, has another theory. He has been investigating UFOs since the 1950s and is convinced there is a link between the two. He suggests that the genuine formations are created by an energy that is not used on this planet. He has also discovered, with the help of a specialized computer program, that the crop circles are capable of making an unusual kind of music.

Whatever the cause of the phenomenon, one thing is clear. The attraction of crop circles is the mystery surrounding them. Once the mystery has been solved, they will cease to be interesting.

Before reading: Travel

1 **Match a word in box A with a word in box B to make tourism and travel phrases.**

A	B
package	weekend
seaside	flight
long-haul	town
long	holiday

A	B
budget	trip
exotic	tour
coach	destination
day	airline

2 **Complete the sentences with the phrases from exercise 1.**

1 My parents like having everything organized for them, so every year they book a ______________.
2 When we were young we always went on holiday to a ______________ near the beach.
3 Sometimes you need to have some injections before you go on holiday to an ______________.
4 My grandparents prefer going on a ______________ so they can see everything from their seats.
5 Last year we went on a ______________ to Australia. We were on board for over 24 hours!
6 Last year we flew to Amsterdam with a ______________. It was really cheap!
7 We didn't want to go away last summer so we often went on a ______________ from home.
8 Last month we spent a ______________ in the mountains. We came home on Monday evening.

3 **Read the text about low-cost airlines and match the headings (1–6) with the paragraphs (A–E). There is one heading that you do not need.**

1 Paperless operations
2 Travelling without tickets
3 Online booking
4 Reduced number of flight attendants
5 Efficient use of airports and aircraft
6 No free lunch

CHALLENGE!

Find out which budget airlines fly from Britain to your country and which airports they use. Make notes on the airline, the schedules and the prices for the airport nearest to you.

____
____
____
____

Budget air travel

Budget air travel has made travelling abroad much more popular than it ever has been before. But how do airlines like easyJet and Ryanair manage to cut their prices and still remain competitive? Listed below are the main methods used for cutting costs.

A ______________

Booking over the internet reduces the need for a call centre, and eliminates the use of a travel agent in the purchasing of tickets. More than 95% of easyJet seats are now sold online and all planes have been painted with the web address of the airline.

B ______________

Airlines have reduced the time the aircraft spend in airports between landing and take-off so that more journeys can be made every day. Ryanair often uses secondary airports whose fees are cheaper than main airports.

C ______________

Passengers are only required to present their passports and booking confirmation at the check-in desk, which eliminates the cost of issuing tickets. Instead of a ticket, passengers receive an email containing their flight details and booking reference.

D ______________

Passengers are not offered an onboard meal by low-cost airlines, whose reasoning is that passengers would only complain about it anyway! In this way, management and bureaucracy charges are reduced, and passengers are not obliged to pay for something they don't want.

E ______________

As well as eliminating the need to issue flight tickets for passengers, low-cost airlines have invested in high-tech computer applications for their staff, reducing the paper consumption in their offices.

Before reading: Advertising

1 Complete the summary of the text on page 93 of the Student's Book with the words in the box.

brand consumers firms income promote purchase sponsors supply target vouchers

The text questions how ethical it is for advertisers to [1]________ schoolchildren in their campaigns. Large [2]________ provide sports equipment to schools with the aim of capturing the children as the [3]________ of the future. The names of the [4]________ are written in big letters on the clothes. Other companies offer computer equipment in exchange for [5]________. All of them are trying to encourage the children to be loyal to their [6]________.

Another advertising strategy is practised by food and drinks companies. They [7]________ vending machines to schools where children can [8]________snacks at break time. Parents say these machines only serve to [9]________ unhealthy eating, but the money schools earn from them provides them with an [10]________ of over £10,000.

2 Read the text about Jamie Oliver and choose the best answers.

1 'Feed Me Better' is the name of
  a a cookery programme.
  b a cookery book.
  c a campaign against bad eating habits.
  d a campaign run by the government.
2 Jamie Oliver is
  a the presenter of a TV programme.
  b a cook in an expensive restaurant.
  c a cookery teacher in a school.
  d the head cook in a school canteen.
3 Jamie Oliver discovered that school dinners were
  a bought from local shops.
  b not made from natural ingredients.
  c not cooked properly.
  d too expensive for parents.
4 Nora Sands, the dinner lady, wanted to
  a spend more money on food.
  b save money on food.
  c appear on TV.
  d give the children better food.
5 Since 2005, school dinners have
  a improved.
  b become more expensive.
  c become cheaper.
  d become bigger.

'Feed Me Better'

'Feed Me Better' is the name of the campaign run by TV chef, Jamie Oliver, to improve eating habits in British schools. Jamie is popular with young people all over Britain because of his cookery programmes. His ingredients are fresh, his recipes are simple, and his meals are absolutely delicious.

So when he found out what Britain's schoolchildren were eating at school, he went on the warpath. He discovered that school dinners centred around processed food, chips and burgers, and that children were incapable of recognizing basic vegetables. So Jamie resolved to do something about it.

He decided to make a TV series called *Jamie's School Dinners* which showed the successes and failures of his attempt to improve the dinner menu of a school in Greenwich, London. He was assisted by the school dinner lady, Nora Sands, who was keen to learn how to give the children a more balanced meal while not exceeding her budget.

At the same time as the programmes were being filmed, Jamie ran a national campaign called 'Feed Me Better' to bring the state of the nation's school dinners to the attention of the government.

As a result of the 300,000-signature petition that Jamie presented to Prime Minister Tony Blair in the spring of 2005, new legislation was brought in to control school dinners. Now children are promised two pieces of fruit with their meal, and fizzy drinks, sweets, chocolate and crisps are banned.

Jamie Oliver has shown that it is possible to do something positive for Britain's schoolchildren instead of just using them to make money.

CHALLENGE!

Design a school dinner menu with three different choices of starter, main course and dessert.

____

____

____

____

FUNCTIONS BANK

Talking about photos
This photo's [from our summer holiday].
There's a boy at the back / at the front.
There's a girl on the left / on the right / in the foreground / in the background.
It looks as though / as if / like [you're enjoying yourselves].

Narrating events
When I was six, [I went to the theatre] for the first time
I remember [my first day at school].
One day [I stayed at school for lunch].
At first [it was fun].
After a few minutes [it started to rain].
A few minutes later [the telephone rang].
Later on [we started dancing].
After that [I never spoke to him again].
In the end [we got home safely].
Finally [I told my parents everything].

A job interview
How did you find out about the job?
Have you worked [in a shop] before?
Why do you think you're the right person for the job?
We'll be in touch by the end of next week.
I saw your advert [in the local newspaper].
I served customers, I made phone calls, I cleaned.
I'm hard-working and reliable.

At the Doctor's
What can I do for you?
How long have you been feeling like this?
I'll just take your temperature.
I'll prescribe [some antibiotics].
Take the tablets three times a day after meals.
I've got a temperature and a bad cough.
I haven't been feeling very well recently.
I've got a sore throat / a headache / an upset stomach.

Talking about plans
Have you got any plans [for the weekend]?
Are you busy [at the weekend]?
I'm going to have an early night.
What are you doing on [Sunday]?
What about [Sunday evening]?

Deciding what to do
Why don't we go to [the theatre]?
Do you fancy going for a walk?
Thanks, but I've already got plans [for Saturday].
It's kind of you to ask, but I'm busy [on Sunday].
I don't fancy [going out for a walk].
You'll enjoy it when you get there.
OK. You've persuaded me.

Making conversations
Excuse me. You're [Ben Wilson's sister], aren't you?
We've met somewhere before, haven't we?
How do you know [Ben]?
What about you? Have you got any hobbies?
What kinds of [films] do you like?
Anyway, I'd better get back to my friends.
Nice talking to you.
See you around.

Asking for information
Hello. I wonder if you could help me?
Can you tell me where [the nearest post office] is?
Would you mind telling me if the plane is on time?
Do you know which platform the trains [to London] go from?

Arguing your case
Do you really think so?
I don't think that's a very good idea.
Are you sure about that?
I take your point, but on the other hand ...
I see what you mean, but ...
I suppose you could be right.
OK, whatever you want. I don't feel strongly about it.
Well, if that's what you really want to do, then OK.
Oh, I don't agree.
I'm not convinced.

Evaluating an experience
What was [the play] like?
I loved every minute of it.
The actors were awesome.
He was such a brilliant actor.
It was so awful.
The male and female leads were both atrocious.

Informal letter

Dear Michelle,

Thanks for your letter. It was great to hear from you and to hear about your skiing trip. I'm glad you had a good time!

I've taken so long to write back because I've been busy studying for my exams. They're over now, and I think I've passed everything, except physics, of course.

How about you? Have you finished your exams yet? Perhaps we can get together when school finishes. If you want to come down to Bristol for a weekend in July, it would be great to see you. Tell me what you think.

The only other news is that my brother Andrew has got engaged. His fiancée is quite nice actually, and I think we're going to get on really well.

Anyway, that's all for now. Please write soon and tell me when you can come and visit.

Best wishes,

Jane

PS If you can't come to Bristol, I don't mind travelling up to Manchester.

- Start the letter with *Dear* and your friend's first name.
- You can use informal language.
- You can use contractions.
- You can use phrasal verbs.
- Use a phrase to bring your letter to a close.
- End your letter with *Best wishes*.
- If you want to introduce some more information or something you have forgotten you can put *PS* (postscript) after your name.

Essay (for and against)

There are few people today who could exist without their mobile phones. Nevertheless, the invention of the mobile phone also has its drawbacks that people tend to forget about.

Not all people know how to use a mobile phone with sufficient respect, and trying to sleep on public transport these days has become impossible. Family visits have also lost out as younger members spend the afternoon texting friends or playing games when in earlier days they would have been interacting with the rest of the family.

However, there is no denying that mobile phones have a number of advantages. Parents with teenagers give their children more freedom if they take their phones with them when they go out. In addition, the mobile is useful for teenagers for getting home as all they have to do is dial their parents' number and the family taxi will arrive at the arranged time free of charge.

On balance, it seems that mobile phones have as many disadvantages as positive aspects. However, in some situations they are indispensable. If you have a car accident on a lonely road in the middle of the night, it's clear that the quickest way to solve the problem is by making a phone call. In this way I, for one, am happier with my mobile phone in my bag, than without it, and I would recommend every driver to carry a phone with them at all times.

- Divide your essay into four paragraphs.
- Write an interesting introduction to your essay that will encourage your reader to continue reading.
- In the second paragraph include points against your argument.
- In the third paragraph include points in favour of your argument.
- The fourth paragraph should be a conclusion balancing the arguments for and against.
- Use linking expressions (see circled examples) to guide your reader through your essay.

Formal letter

- Start *Dear Sir or Madam* if you don't know the name of the person you are writing to. Use the person's title (*Mr, Mrs, Ms*) and their surname if you do.
- Use formal expressions.
- Avoid contractions.
- State your reason for writing in the first paragraph.
- State your requests using indirect questions.
- Use a phrase to bring your letter to a close.
- End your letter with *Yours faithfully* if you started with *Dear Sir or Madam*, and *Yours sincerely* if you started with the person's title and surname.
- Sign your name and print it in full afterwards.

Dear Sir or Madam,

I am writing to enquire about the holiday apartments on the Costa Brava advertised in Beach Holidays magazine this month.

In your advertisement you mention that all the apartments are self-catering. Would you mind telling me what cooking facilities are available in the kitchen? Could you also tell me if cooking utensils are provided?

I noticed from your advertisement that the beach is very near. However, I would also like to know if the apartments have a swimming pool as we will be travelling with small children.

I would be very grateful if you could send me a list of apartments and prices with a view to making a reservation in August.

I look forward to hearing from you.

Yours faithfully,

Catherine Archer

MS CATHERINE ARCHER

Essay (giving your opinion)

There is a saying that "travel broadens the mind" and it is certainly true that you can learn a lot from visiting other countries. In my opinion, travelling helps you to improve your language skills, increase your awareness of the world and become more independent.

Travelling allows you to practise your foreign language skills in real situations, rather than just in a classroom. For example, you will almost certainly need to buy tickets, book accommodation and order food and drink. Moreover, you are likely to find yourself meeting people and making conversation in a foreign language. These encounters can sometimes lead to lasting friendships, too.

People who have never left their hometown may have quite a narrow view of the world. In contrast, people who have travelled can base their opinions on a wider range of experiences. Furthermore, travelling can raise your awareness of important global issues. For instance, visiting the Amazonian rainforest will probably make you more passionate about protecting it from destruction.

Travelling puts you in situations which you do not find in your normal everyday routine at home. Learning how to cope with these is good experience, and makes you a stronger and more independent person. For example, young people who backpack around Europe often have to learn how to live cheaply while they are travelling.

In conclusion, I would say that travelling is a very valuable experience. It provides a form of education which you cannot get from books or in the classroom.

- Write an interesting introduction outlining the general areas you are going to cover in your essay.
- Allocate one paragraph to each general area.
- Include examples (see underlined phrases) to illustrate your points.
- Use linking expressions (see circled examples) to connect points, where necessary.
- The final paragraph should be a conclusion summing up your opinion in different words and including a final thought on the issue.

a blue moon /ə ˌbluː ˈmuːn/
a red herring /ə ˌred ˈherɪŋ/
a white lie /ə ˌwaɪt ˈlaɪ/
against the law /əˌgenst ðə ˈlɔː/
alpaca /ælˈpækə/
ankle-length /ˈæŋkl ˌleŋθ/
appear /əˈpɪə(r)/
appearance /əˈpɪərəns/
assist /əˈsɪst/
assistance /əˈsɪstəns/
attach /əˈtætʃ/
attached /əˈtætʃt/
attachment /əˈtætʃmənt/
baggy /ˈbægi/
bank account /ˈbæŋk əˌkaʊnt/
behaviour /bɪˈheɪvjə(r)/
boots /buːts/
cash machine /ˈkæʃ məˌʃiːn/
checked /tʃekt/
citizen /ˈsɪtɪzn/
confront /kənˈfrʌnt/
cotton /ˈkɒtn/
credit card /ˈkredɪt ˌkɑːd/
decorated /ˈdekəreɪtɪd/
detect /dɪˈtekt/
detection /dɪˈtekʃn/
deter /dɪˈtɜː(r)/
develop /dɪˈveləp/
development /dɪˈveləpmənt/
download /ˈdaʊnləʊd/
dress /dres/
exasperate /ɪgˈzæspəreɪt/
exasperation /ɪgzæspəˈreɪʃn/
exchange student /ɪksˈtʃeɪndʒ ˌstjuːdnt/
facilities /fəˈsɪlətiz/
fine /faɪn/
fully-equipped /ˌfʊli ɪˈkwɪpt/
fur /fɜː(r)/
fur-lined /ˈfɜː ˌlaɪnd/
gape /geɪp/
glance /glɑːns/
glare /gleə(r)/
green fingers /ˌgriːn ˈfɪŋgəz/
harass /ˈhærəs/
harassment /həˈræsmənt/
hard /hɑːd/
headscarf /ˈhedskɑːf/
illegal /ɪˈliːgl/
improvement /ɪmˈpruːvmənt/
in black and white /ɪn ˌblæk ənd ˈwaɪt/
in contact /ɪn ˈkɒntækt/
in theory /ɪn ˈθɪəri/
initially /ɪˈnɪʃəli/
interact /ɪntərˈækt/
investigate /ɪnˈvestɪgeɪt/
investigation /ɪnvestɪˈgeɪʃn/
kilt /kɪlt/
kimono /kɪˈməʊnəʊ/
knee-length /ˈniː ˌleŋθ/
linen /ˈlɪnɪn/
long-sleeved /ˌlɒŋ ˈsliːvd/
look (at) /ˈlʊk (ˌæt, ət)/
look like /ˈlʊk ˌlaɪk/
loose /luːs/
manage /ˈmænɪdʒ/
matching /ˈmætʃɪŋ/
material /məˈtɪəriəl/
misuse /mɪsˈjuːs/
monitor /ˈmɒnɪtə(r)/
necessarily /ˌnesəˈserəli/
observe /əbˈzɜːv/
offender /əˈfendə(r)/
ordinary people /ˈɔːdnri ˌpiːpl/
parka /ˈpɑːkə/
patterned /ˈpætnd/
peek /piːk/

/i/ happy	/æ/ flag	/ɜː/ her	/ʊ/ look	/ʌ/ mum	/ɔɪ/ noisy	/ɪə/ here
/ɪ/ it	/ɑː/ art	/ɒ/ not	/uː/ you	/eɪ/ day	/aʊ/ how	/eə/ wear
/iː/ he	/e/ egg	/ɔː/ four	/ə/ sugar	/aɪ/ why	/əʊ/ go	/ʊə/ tourist

peer /pɪə(r)/ ______
plain 🔑 /pleɪn/ ______
poncho /ˈpɒntʃəʊ/ ______
potential 🔑 /pəˈtenʃl/ ______
privacy /ˈprɪvəsi/ ______
put the price up (of sth) 🔑 /ˌpʊt ðə ˈpraɪs ˌʌp (əv ...)/ ______
recognition 🔑 /rekəgˈnɪʃn/ ______
recognize 🔑 /ˈrekəgnaɪz/ ______
rely on 🔑 /rɪˈlaɪ ˌɒn/ ______
safe from 🔑 /ˈseɪf frəm/ ______
sandals /ˈsændlz/ ______
sari /ˈsɑːri/ ______
satellite /ˈsætəlaɪt/ ______
seal skin /ˈsiːl ˌskɪn/ ______
secretively /ˈsiːkrətɪvli/ ______
secretly 🔑 /ˈsiːkrətli/ ______
security 🔑 /sɪˈkjʊərəti/ ______
see 🔑 /siː/ ______
shape 🔑 /ʃeɪp/ ______
shoplifter /ˈʃɒplɪftə(r)/ ______
short-sleeved /ˌʃɔːt ˈsliːvd/ ______
soft 🔑 /sɒft/ ______
software 🔑 /ˈsɒftweə(r)/ ______
spot 🔑 /spɒt/ ______
stare 🔑 /steə(r)/ ______
stay in contact 🔑 /ˌsteɪ ɪn ˈkɒntækt/ ______
stripy /ˈstraɪpi/ ______
strong 🔑 /strɒŋ/ ______
surveillance /səˈveɪləns/ ______
tag /tæg/ ______
tartan /ˈtɑːtn/ ______
texture /ˈtekstʃə(r)/ ______
that sort of (money) 🔑 /ˈðæt ˌsɔːt əv (ˌmʌni)/ ______
the golden rule /ðə ˌgəʊldən ˈruːl/ ______
thick 🔑 /θɪk/ ______
tight 🔑 /taɪt/ ______
treat 🔑 /triːt/ ______
treatment 🔑 /ˈtriːtmənt/ ______
tunic /ˈtjuːnɪk/ ______
turban /ˈtɜːbən/ ______
upgrade /ʌpˈgreɪd/ ______
vulnerable /ˈvʌlnərəbl/ ______
warn 🔑 /wɔːn/ ______
watch 🔑 /wɒtʃ/ ______
wide 🔑 /waɪd/ ______
wooden 🔑 /ˈwʊdn/ ______
work out 🔑 /ˌwɜːk ˈaʊt/ ______

Additional vocabulary

/p/ **p**en	/d/ **d**og	/tʃ/ bea**ch**	/v/ **v**ery	/s/ **s**peak	/ʒ/ televi**s**ion	/n/ **n**ow	/r/ **r**adio
/b/ **b**ig	/k/ **c**an	/dʒ/ **j**ob	/θ/ **th**ink	/z/ **z**oo	/h/ **h**ouse	/ŋ/ si**ng**	/j/ **y**es
/t/ **t**wo	/g/ **g**ood	/f/ **f**ood	/ð/ **th**en	/ʃ/ **sh**e	/m/ **m**eat	/l/ **l**ate	/w/ **w**e

VOCABULARY NOTEBOOK UNIT 2

accurate /'ækjərət/
admit /əd'mɪt/
amnesia /æm'niːziə/
amused /ə'mjuːzd/
apologize /ə'pɒlədʒaɪz/
apparently /ə'pærəntli/
arrogant /'ærəgənt/
ashamed of /ə'ʃeɪmd əv/
at once /ət 'wʌns/
baffled /'bæfld/
bored with /'bɔːd wɪð/
boredom /'bɔːdəm/
boring /'bɔːrɪŋ/
break down /ˌbreɪk 'daʊn/
burst into tears /ˌbɜːst ˌɪntə 'tɪəz/
challenge sb to sth /'tʃælɪndʒ ˌ... tə ˌ.../
clean up /ˌkliːn 'ʌp/
close friend /ˌkləʊs 'frend/
come back /ˌkʌm 'bæk/
communicative /kə'mjuːnɪkətɪv/
confused /kən'fjuːzd/
confusing /kən'fjuːzɪŋ/
confusion /kən'fjuːʒn/
cope /kəʊp/
deep (adj) /diːp/
delighted /dɪ'laɪtɪd/
depict /dɪ'pɪkt/
depressed /dɪ'prest/
depression /dɪ'preʃn/
diagnose /'daɪəgnəʊz/
disappointed /dɪsə'pɔɪntɪd/
disappointing /dɪsə'pɔɪntɪŋ/
disappointment /dɪsə'pɔɪntmənt/
discharge /dɪs'tʃɑːdʒ/
dismayed /dɪs'meɪd/
downturn /'daʊntɜːn/
driving test /'draɪvɪŋ ˌtest/

earliest memory /ˌɜːliəst 'meməri/
easy-going /ˌiːzi 'gəʊɪŋ/
ecstatic /ɪk'stætɪk/
embarrassed /ɪm'bærəst/
embarrassing /ɪm'bærəsɪŋ/
embarrassment /ɪm'bærəsmənt/
enrol /ɪn'rəʊl/
enthusiasm (n) /ɪn'θjuːziæzəm/
escort /ɪ'skɔːt/
ethnic minority /ˌeθnɪk maɪ'nɒrəti/
even though /'iːvn ˌðəʊ/
extrovert /'ekstrəvɜːt/
fall through /ˌfɔːl 'θruː/
fast-moving /ˌfɑːst 'muːvɪŋ/
fed up /ˌfed 'ʌp/
fetch /fetʃ/
flip-flop /'flɪp ˌflɒp/
fluent /'fluːənt/
formal /'fɔːml/
furious /'fjʊəriəs/
fury /'fjʊəri/
general knowledge /ˌdʒenrəl 'nɒlɪdʒ/
generous /'dʒenərəs/
get to know sb /ˌget tə 'nəʊ .../
get up /ˌget 'ʌp/
give up /ˌgɪv 'ʌp/
gloomy /'gluːmi/
go out /ˌgəʊ 'aʊt/
go up /ˌgəʊ 'ʌp/
grow up /ˌgrəʊ 'ʌp/
guilty /'gɪlti/
happy with /'hæpi wɪð/
hold on /ˌhəʊld 'ɒn/
homesick /'həʊmsɪk/
homesickness /'həʊmsɪknəs/
irritated /'ɪrɪteɪtɪd/
jealous /'dʒeləs/

/i/ happy	/æ/ flag	/ɜː/ her	/ʊ/ look	/ʌ/ mum	/ɔɪ/ noisy	/ɪə/ here
/ɪ/ it	/ɑː/ art	/ɒ/ not	/uː/ you	/eɪ/ day	/aʊ/ how	/eə/ wear
/iː/ he	/e/ egg	/ɔː/ four	/ə/ sugar	/aɪ/ why	/əʊ/ go	/ʊə/ tourist

laugh out loud /ˌlɑːf aʊt ˈlaʊd/

look for (phr vb) /ˈlʊk ˌfɔː(r), fə(r)/

lose your memory /ˌluːz jɔː ˈmeməri/

loss /lɒs/

memorabilia /memərəˈbɪliə/

memorial /məˈmɔːriəl/

memory loss /ˈmeməri ˌlɒs/

memory /ˈmeməri/

modest /ˈmɒdɪst/

nervous about /ˈnɜːvəs (əˌbaʊt)/

nervousness /ˈnɜːvəsnəs/

not have time to do sth /ˌnɒt hæv ˌtaɪm tə ˈduː ˌ.../

on your way home /ˌɒn jɔː ˌweɪ ˈhəʊm/

once /wʌns/

outgoing /ˈaʊtgəʊɪŋ/

patchy /ˈpætʃi/

patriotic /pætriˈɒtɪk/

petrified /ˈpetrɪfaɪd/

phrase book /ˈfreɪz ˌbʊk/

pirate (n) /ˈpaɪrət/

pleased /pliːzd/

portray /pɔːˈtreɪ/

possessions /pəˈzeʃnz/

proud of /ˈpraʊd əv/

rarely /ˈreəli/

relieved /rɪˈliːvd/

remembrance /rɪˈmembrəns/

reminder /rɪˈmaɪndə(r)/

reserved /rɪˈzɜːvd/

resign /rɪˈzaɪn/

rucksack /ˈrʌksæk/

run out of sth /ˌrʌn ˈaʊt əv ˌ.../

scared of /ˈskeəd əv/

scrawl /skrɔːl/

sensitive /ˈsensətɪv/

set off /ˌset ˈɒf/

severity /sɪˈverəti/

short notice /ˌʃɔːt ˈnəʊtɪs/

show your emotions /ˌʃəʊ jɔːr ɪˈməʊʃnz/

since /sɪns/

skull /skʌl/

souvenir /suːvəˈnɪə(r)/

speak up /ˌspiːk ˈʌp/

squire (n) /ˈskwaɪə(r)/

stand up /ˌstænd ˈʌp/

stay in /ˌsteɪ ˈɪn/

stock exchange /ˈstɒk ɪkˌstʃeɪndʒ/

stunning /ˈstʌnɪŋ/

subway /ˈsʌbweɪ/

surprised at /səˈpraɪzd ət/

the norm /ðə ˈnɔːm/

though /ðəʊ/

throw /θrəʊ/

tickets /ˈtɪkɪts/

tired of /ˈtaɪəd əv/

tremble (v) /ˈtrembl/

truly /ˈtruːli/

turn up /ˌtɜːn ˈʌp/

underachievement /ʌndərəˈtʃiːvmənt/

upset about /ʌpˈset əˌbaʊt/

wake up /ˌweɪk ˈʌp/

warm up /ˌwɔːm ˈʌp/

whereas /weərˈæz/

while /waɪl/

without difficulty /wɪˌðaʊt ˈdɪfɪkəlti/

worried about /ˈwʌrid əˌbaʊt/

Additional vocabulary

/p/ **p**en	/d/ **d**og	/tʃ/ bea**ch**	/v/ **v**ery	/s/ **s**peak	/ʒ/ televi**si**on	/n/ **n**ow	/r/ **r**adio
/b/ **b**ig	/k/ **c**an	/dʒ/ **j**ob	/θ/ **th**ink	/z/ **z**oo	/h/ **h**ouse	/ŋ/ si**ng**	/j/ **y**es
/t/ **t**wo	/g/ **g**ood	/f/ **f**ood	/ð/ **th**en	/ʃ/ **sh**e	/m/ **m**eat	/l/ **l**ate	/w/ **w**e

accountant /ə'kaʊntənt/ ____
adapt /ə'dæpt/ ____
application /æplɪ'keɪʃn/ ____
apply for a job /əˌplaɪ fər ə 'dʒɒb/ ____
appropriate /ə'prəʊpriət/ ____
astronaut /'æstrənɔːt/ ____
attend an interview /əˌtend ən 'ɪntəvjuː/ ____
back-breaking /'bæk ˌbreɪkɪŋ/ ____
barrister /'bærɪstə(r)/ ____
be promoted /ˌbi prəʊ'məʊtɪd/ ____
brainstorm ideas /ˌbreɪnstɔːm aɪ'dɪəz/ ____
builder /'bɪldə(r)/ ____
busy /'bɪzi/ ____
call off /ˌkɔːl 'ɒf/ ____
carpenter /'kɑːpɪntə(r)/ ____
catering /'keɪtərɪŋ/ ____
chair meetings /ˌtʃeə 'miːtɪŋz/ ____
challenging /'tʃælɪndʒɪŋ/ ____
child psychologist /ˌtʃaɪld saɪ'kɒlədʒɪst/ ____
civil servant /ˌsɪvl 'sɜːvənt/ ____
coal miner /'kəʊl ˌmaɪnə(r)/ ____
colleague /'kɒliːg/ ____
commitment /kə'mɪtmənt/ ____
complicated /'kɒmplɪkeɪtɪd/ ____
computer literacy /kəmˌpjuːtə 'lɪtərəsi/ ____
consider yourself to be /kən'sɪdə jəˌself tə bi/ ____
considerable /kən'sɪdərəbl/ ____
correspondent /kɒrə'spɒndənt/ ____
councillor /'kaʊnsələ(r)/ ____
deal with customers /ˌdiːl ˌwɪð 'kʌstəməz/ ____
distributor /dɪ'strɪbjətə(r)/ ____
draw up contracts /ˌdrɔːr ʌp 'kɒntrækts/ ____

editor /'edɪtə(r)/ ____
electrician /ɪlek'trɪʃn/ ____
emphasis /'emfəsɪs/ ____
employee /ɪm'plɔɪiː/ ____
encourage sb to do sth /ɪnˌkʌrɪdʒ ... tə 'duː/ ____
engineer /endʒɪ'nɪə(r)/ ____
enjoy a challenge /ɪnˌdʒɔɪ ə 'tʃælɪndʒ/ ____
enthusiastic /ɪnθjuːzi'æstɪk/ ____
environment /ɪn'vaɪrənmənt/ ____
essential /ɪ'senʃl/ ____
excel /ɪk'sel/ ____
experience /ɪk'spɪəriəns/ ____
fill in an application form /ˌfɪl ˌɪn ən æplɪ'keɪʃn ˌfɔːm/ ____
financial analyst /faɪˌnænʃl, fəˌnæ- 'ænəlɪst/ ____
firefighter /'faɪəfaɪtə(r)/ ____
flexible /'fleksəbl/ ____
flight attendant /'flaɪt əˌtendənt/ ____
full training /ˌfʊl 'treɪnɪŋ/ ____
give out /ˌgɪv 'aʊt/ ____
good with numbers /ˌgʊd wɪð 'nʌmbəz/ ____
gradually /'grædʒuəli/ ____
hairdresser /'heədresə(r)/ ____
hand in your resignation /ˌhænd ɪn jɔː rezɪg'neɪʃn/ ____
I would be very grateful /ˌaɪ ˌwʊd ˌbi 'veri ˌgreɪtfl/ ____
illustrator /'ɪləstreɪtə(r)/ ____
in a word /ˌɪn ə 'wɜːd/ ____
in charge of sth/sb /ɪn 'tʃɑːdʒ əv/ ____
in person /ˌɪn 'pɜːsn/ ____
instinctively /ɪn'stɪŋktɪvli/ ____
investment /ɪn'vestmənt/ ____
keep up with new technology /ˌkiːp ˌʌp wɪð ˌnjuː tek'nɒlədʒi/ ____
lawyer /'lɔːjə(r)/ ____

/i/ happy	/æ/ flag	/ɜː/ her	/ʊ/ look	/ʌ/ mum	/ɔɪ/ noisy	/ɪə/ here
/ɪ/ it	/ɑː/ art	/ɒ/ not	/uː/ you	/eɪ/ day	/aʊ/ how	/eə/ wear
/iː/ he	/e/ egg	/ɔː/ four	/ə/ sugar	/aɪ/ why	/əʊ/ go	/ʊə/ tourist

liaise with a team /liˌeɪz wɪð ə ˈtiːm/ ______

look forward to 🔑 /ˌlʊk ˈfɔːwəd tə/ ______

look up 🔑 /ˌlʊk ˈʌp/ ______

lorry driver 🔑 /ˈlɒri ˌdraɪvə(r)/ ______

make sb redundant /ˌmeɪk … rɪˈdʌndənt/ ______

make up 🔑 /ˌmeɪk ˈʌp/ ______

mechanic /məˈkænɪk/ ______

meet deadlines /ˌmiːt ˈdedlaɪnz/ ______

menial /ˈmiːniəl/ ______

monotonous /məˈnɒtənəs/ ______

musician 🔑 /mjuˈzɪʃn/ ______

nanny /ˈnæni/ ______

negotiable /nɪˈɡəʊʃiəbl/ ______

nowadays /ˈnaʊədeɪz/ ______

nurse 🔑 /nɜːs/ ______

nursery school teacher /ˈnɜːsəri ˌskuːl ˌtiːtʃə(r)/ ______

operate machinery 🔑 /ˌɒpəreɪt məˈʃiːnəri/ ______

opportunity 🔑 /ɒpəˈtjuːnəti/ ______

patience 🔑 /ˈpeɪʃns/ ______

photographer 🔑 /fəˈtɒɡrəfə(r)/ ______

pick up 🔑 /ˌpɪk ˈʌp/ ______

pilot 🔑 /ˈpaɪlət/ ______

plumber /ˈplʌmə(r)/ ______

pocket money 🔑 /ˈpɒkɪt ˌmʌni/ ______

politician 🔑 /pɒləˈtɪʃn/ ______

post 🔑 /pəʊst/ ______

prevent 🔑 /prɪˈvent/ ______

promotion 🔑 /prəˈməʊʃn/ ______

put off 🔑 /ˌpʊt ˈɒf/ ______

put out 🔑 /ˌpʊt ˈaʊt/ ______

reference 🔑 /ˈrefrəns/ ______

reliable /rɪˈlaɪəbl/ ______

report on sales figures 🔑 /rɪˌpɔːt ɒn ˈseɪlz ˌfɪɡəz/ ______

requirement 🔑 /rɪˈkwaɪəmənt/ ______

resident 🔑 /ˈrezɪdənt/ ______

responsibility 🔑 /rɪspɒnsəˈbɪləti/ ______

rewarding 🔑 /rɪˈwɔːdɪŋ/ ______

salary 🔑 /ˈsæləri/ ______

scientist 🔑 /ˈsaɪəntɪst/ ______

secretary 🔑 /ˈsekrətri/ ______

sign a contract 🔑 /ˌsaɪn ə ˈkɒntrækt/ ______

skilled 🔑 /skɪld/ ______

skills 🔑 /skɪlz/ ______

solicitor /səˈlɪsɪtə(r)/ ______

specialized knowledge /ˌspeʃəlaɪzd ˈnɒlɪdʒ/ ______

stockbroker /ˈstɒkˌbrəʊkə(r)/ ______

stressful /ˈstresfl/ ______

suitable 🔑 /ˈsuːtəbl/ ______

supply teacher 🔑 /səˈplaɪ ˌtiːtʃə(r)/ ______

surgeon /ˈsɜːdʒən/ ______

take an order 🔑 /ˌteɪk ən ˈɔːdə(r)/ ______

take off 🔑 /ˌteɪk ˈɒf/ ______

tell off 🔑 /ˌtel ˈɒf/ ______

timetable 🔑 /ˈtaɪmteɪbl/ ______

tired of 🔑 /ˈtaɪəd əv/ ______

tough 🔑 /tʌf/ ______

traditionally 🔑 /trəˈdɪʃənəli/ ______

trust 🔑 /trʌst/ ______

turn down 🔑 /ˌtɜːn ˈdaʊn/ ______

underneath 🔑 /ʌndəˈniːθ/ ______

upload data /ˌʌpləʊd ˈdeɪtə/ ______

visor /ˈvaɪzə(r)/ ______

wholesaler /ˈhəʊlseɪlə(r)/ ______

work on an assembly line /ˌwɜːk ˌɒn ən əˈsembli ˌlaɪn/ ______

working arrangements 🔑 /ˈwɜːkɪŋ əˌreɪndʒmənts/ ______

/p/ **p**en	/d/ **d**og	/tʃ/ **b**ea**ch**	/v/ **v**ery	/s/ **s**peak	/ʒ/ televi**s**ion	/n/ **n**ow	/r/ **r**adio
/b/ **b**ig	/k/ **c**an	/dʒ/ **j**ob	/θ/ **th**ink	/z/ **z**oo	/h/ **h**ouse	/ŋ/ si**ng**	/j/ **y**es
/t/ **t**wo	/g/ **g**ood	/f/ **f**ood	/ð/ **th**en	/ʃ/ **sh**e	/m/ **m**eat	/l/ **l**ate	/w/ **w**e

achievement /ə'tʃi:vmənt/

activate /'æktɪveɪt/

active /'æktɪv/

alien /'eɪliən/

alienate /'eɪliəneɪt/

ankle /'æŋkl/

apply /ə'plaɪ/

article /'ɑ:tɪkl/

assign /ə'saɪn/

associate /ə'səʊʃieɪt, -sieɪt/

benefit /'benəfɪt/

bite sb's head off /ˌbaɪt ... 'hed ɒf/

blame /bleɪm/

break /breɪk/

breathing apparatus /'bri:ðɪŋ æpəˌreɪtəs/

catapult /'kætəpʌlt/

chain (n) /tʃeɪn/

chord /kɔ:d/

claim /kleɪm/

clarify /'klærɪfaɪ/

clear /klɪə(r)/

clear (your) throat /ˌklɪə ... 'θrəʊt/

cold-blooded /ˌkəʊld 'blʌdɪd/

cord /kɔ:d/

cross (your) fingers /ˌkrɒs ... 'fɪŋgəz/

deduce /dɪ'dju:s/

depending on /dɪ'pendɪŋ ˌɒn/

diabetes /daɪə'bi:ti:z/

different /'dɪfrənt/

differentiate /dɪfə'renʃieɪt/

dislocate /'dɪsləkeɪt/

draft /drɑ:ft/

draught /drɑ:ft/

dull /dʌl/

end-of-term exams /ˌend əv ˌtɜ:m ɪg'zæmz/

Enough of all that /ɪ'nʌf əv ˌɔ:l ˌðæt/

essentially /ɪ'senʃəli/

ever again /ˌevər ə'gen/

example /ɪg'zɑ:mpl/

exemplify /ɪg'zemplɪfaɪ/

extreme sport /ɪkˌstri:m 'spɔ:t/

fair-haired /'feə ˌheəd/

fast food /ˌfɑ:st 'fu:d/

fiercely (adv) /'fɪəsli/

file (n) /faɪl/

get cold feet /ˌget ˌkəʊld 'fi:t/

get sth off your chest /ˌget .. ˌɒf jɔ: 'tʃest/

gracefully /'greɪsfəli/

grave (n) /greɪv/

gravestone (n) /'greɪvstəʊn/

green-eyed /'gri:n ˌaɪd/

Guess what? /'ges wɒt/

have a good effect on sth /ˌhæv ə ˌgʊd ɪ'fekt ˌɒn/

have lessons /ˌhæv 'lesnz/

health problem /'helθ ˌprɒbləm/

high blood pressure /ˌhaɪ 'blʌd ˌpreʃə(r)/

high-fat food /'haɪ ˌfæt ˌfu:d/

historical /hɪ'stɒrɪkl/

hold your breath /ˌhəʊld jɔ: 'breθ/

improve your memory /ɪmˌpru:v jɔ: 'meməri/

injury /'ɪndʒəri/

inspire /ɪn'spaɪə(r)/

iron (n) /'aɪən/

junk food /'dʒʌŋk ˌfu:d/

keep an eye on sb / sth /ˌki:p ən 'aɪ ˌɒn/

kind-hearted /ˌkaɪnd 'hɑ:tɪd/

knowledge /'nɒlɪdʒ/

leak /li:k/

leek /li:k/

level-headed /ˌlevl 'hedɪd/

lifestyle /'laɪfstaɪl/

/i/ happ**y**	/æ/ fl**a**g	/ɜ:/ h**er**	/ʊ/ l**oo**k	/ʌ/ m**u**m	/ɔɪ/ n**oi**sy	/ɪə/ h**ere**
/ɪ/ **i**t	/ɑ:/ **ar**t	/ɒ/ n**o**t	/u:/ y**ou**	/eɪ/ d**ay**	/aʊ/ h**ow**	/eə/ w**ear**
/i:/ h**e**	/e/ **e**gg	/ɔ:/ f**our**	/ə/ sug**ar**	/aɪ/ wh**y**	/əʊ/ g**o**	/ʊə/ t**our**ist

maize /meɪz/
manoeuvre /mə'nuːvə(r)/
mare /meə(r)/
mayor 🔑 /meə(r)/
maze /meɪz/
memorize /'meməraɪz/
memory 🔑 /'meməri/
mislead sb /mɪs'liːd/
moose /muːs/
mousse /muːs/
narrow-minded /ˌnærəʊ 'maɪndɪd/
neck 🔑 /nek/
nod (your) head 🔑 /nɒd ... 'hed/
nutritious /nju'trɪʃəs/
obese /əʊ'biːs/
obesity /əʊ'biːsəti/
obstacle /'ɒbstəkl/
occasion 🔑 /ə'keɪʒn/
open-minded /ˌəʊpən 'maɪndɪd/
pantry /'pæntri/
physical exercise 🔑 /ˌfɪzɪkl 'eksəsaɪz/
play it by ear 🔑 /ˌpleɪ ˌɪt ˌbaɪ 'ɪə(r)/
poke (your) nose into sth /ˌpəʊk ... 'nəʊz ˌɪntə/
privately 🔑 /'praɪvətli/
public 🔑 /'pʌblɪk/
publicize /'pʌblɪsaɪz/
pull a muscle 🔑 /ˌpʊl ə 'mʌsl/
pull sb's leg 🔑 /ˌpʊl ... 'leg/
put (your) foot in it 🔑 /ˌpʊt ... 'fʊt ɪn ˌɪt/
raise (your) eyebrows /ˌreɪz ... 'aɪbraʊz/
rehearse /rɪ'hɜːs/
right-handed /ˌraɪt 'hændɪd/
roast (v) /rəʊst/
scary /'skeəri/
session 🔑 /'seʃn/
short-sighted /ˌʃɔːt 'saɪtɪd/
shrug (your) shoulders /ˌʃrʌg ... 'ʃəʊldəz/
simple 🔑 /'sɪmpl/
simplify /'sɪmplɪfaɪ/
split hairs 🔑 /ˌsplɪt 'heəz/
staff 🔑 /stɑːf/
stomach 🔑 /'stʌmək/
stumble /'stʌmbl/
sugary /'ʃʊgəri/
sundial /'sʌndaɪəl/
takeaway meal /ˌteɪkəweɪ 'miːl/
tap (your) foot 🔑 /ˌtæp ... 'fʊt/
tear 🔑 /tɪə(r)/
technique 🔑 /tek'niːk/
That's all for now 🔑 /ˌðæts 'ɔːl fə ˌnaʊ/
thick-skinned /ˌθɪk 'skɪnd/
tier /tɪə(r)/
TV dinner 🔑 /ˌtiː ˌviː 'dɪnə(r)/
twist an ankle 🔑 /ˌtwɪst ən 'æŋkl/
twist sb's arm 🔑 /ˌtwɪst ... 'ɑːm/
understand the gist of sth /ʌndəˌstænd ðə 'dʒɪst əv .../
unusual 🔑 /ʌn'juːʒuəl/
upset stomach 🔑 /ˌʌpset 'stʌmək/
visual /'vɪʒuəl/
visualize /'vɪʒuəlaɪz/
weigh 🔑 /weɪ/
What have you been up to? 🔑 /ˌwɒt həv ˌjuː ˌbiːn 'ʌp ˌtuː/
Why don't we ...? 🔑 /'waɪ ˌdəʊnt ˌwiː /
yoga class /'jəʊgə ˌklɑːs/
yoke /jəʊk/
yolk /jəʊk/

/p/ **p**en	/d/ **d**og	/tʃ/ bea**ch**	/v/ **v**ery	/s/ **s**peak	/ʒ/ televi**s**ion	/n/ **n**ow	/r/ **r**adio
/b/ **b**ig	/k/ **c**an	/dʒ/ **j**ob	/θ/ **th**ink	/z/ **z**oo	/h/ **h**ouse	/ŋ/ si**ng**	/j/ **y**es
/t/ **t**wo	/g/ **g**ood	/f/ **f**ood	/ð/ **th**en	/ʃ/ **sh**e	/m/ **m**eat	/l/ **l**ate	/w/ **w**e

access information /ˌækses ɪnfəˈmeɪʃn/

acid rain /ˌæsɪd ˈreɪn/

advance /ədˈvɑːns/

adventurous /ədˈventʃərəs/

air conditioning /ˈeə kənˌdɪʃənɪŋ/

amount /əˈmaʊnt/

auto- /ˈɔːtəʊ/

be pessimistic about sth /ˌbi pesɪˈmɪstɪk əˌbaʊt .../

best-selling /ˈbest ˌselɪŋ/

biometric /baɪəˈmetrɪk/

burn /bɜːn/

carbon emissions /ˈkɑːbən ɪˌmɪʃnz/

catastrophe /kəˈtæstrəfi/

cause sth to happen /ˌkɔːz ... tə ˈhæpən/

chat room /ˈtʃæt ˌruːm/

climate change /ˈklaɪmət ˌtʃeɪndʒ/

co- /kəʊ/

coal-burning /ˈkəʊl ˌbɜːnɪŋ/

coastal /ˈkəʊstl/

colony /ˈkɒləni/

comet /ˈkɒmɪt/

cordless /ˈkɔːdləs/

damage /ˈdæmɪdʒ/

digital /ˈdɪdʒɪtl/

do research /ˌduː rɪˈsɜːtʃ, ˈriːsɜːtʃ/

download /daʊnˈləʊd/

eco-friendly /ˈiːkəʊ ˌfrendli/

endangered species /ɪnˌdeɪndʒəd ˈspiːʃiːz/

extinction /ɪkˈstɪŋkʃn/

fail to do sth /ˌfeɪl tə ˈduː .../

fifty years on /ˌfɪfti ˌjɪəz ˈɒn/

find out /ˌfaɪnd ˈaʊt/

flock /flɒk/

genetic code /dʒəˌnetɪk ˈkəʊd/

genome /ˈdʒiːnəʊm/

global warming /ˌgləʊbl ˈwɔːmɪŋ/

greenhouse effect /ˈgriːnhaʊs ɪˌfekt/

hard disk /ˌhɑːd ˈdɪsk/

harmful /ˈhɑːmfl/

heat up /ˌhiːt ˈʌp/

illness /ˈɪlnəs/

in conclusion /ˌɪn kənˈkluːʒn/

innovative /ˈɪnəvətɪv/

interpret /ɪnˈtɜːprɪt/

labour-saving /ˈleɪbə ˌseɪvɪŋ/

life expectancy /ˈlaɪf ɪkˌspektənsi/

lifespan /ˈlaɪfspæn/

life-threatening /ˈlaɪf ˌθretənɪŋ/

limb /lɪm/

make a discovery /ˌmeɪk ə dɪˈskʌvəri/

make mistakes /ˌmeɪk mɪˈsteɪks/

malfunction /mælˈfʌŋkʃn/

meet /miːt/

micro- /ˈmaɪkrəʊ/

mono- /ˈmɒnəʊ/

move away from home /ˌmuːv əˌweɪ frəm ˈhəʊm/

multi /ˈmʌlti/

overcrowd /əʊvəˈkraʊd/

ozone layer /ˈəʊzəʊn ˌleɪə(r)/

particularly good at ... /pəˈtɪkjələli ˌgʊd ət/

polar /ˈpəʊlə(r)/

population explosion /pɒpjuˈleɪʃn ɪkˌspləʊʒn/

pre- /priː/

prescribe /prɪˈskraɪb/

prevent /prɪˈvent/

provide /prəˈvaɪd/

qualify /ˈkwɒlɪfaɪ/

rainforest /ˈreɪnfɒrɪst/

/i/ happy	/æ/ flag	/ɜː/ her	/ʊ/ look	/ʌ/ mum	/ɔɪ/ noisy	/ɪə/ here
/ɪ/ it	/ɑː/ art	/ɒ/ not	/uː/ you	/eɪ/ day	/aʊ/ how	/eə/ wear
/iː/ he	/e/ egg	/ɔː/ four	/ə/ sugar	/aɪ/ why	/əʊ/ go	/ʊə/ tourist

reason ⊸ /ˈriːzn/ ________

reduce ⊸ /rɪˈdjuːs/ ________

regenerate /riːˈdʒenəreɪt/ ________

renewable energy /rɪˌnjuːəbl ˈenədʒi/ ________

result in ⊸ /rɪˈzʌlt ˌɪn/ ________

retire ⊸ /rɪˈtaɪə(r)/ ________

search engine ⊸ /ˈsɜːtʃ ˌendʒɪn/ ________

self-supporting /ˌself səˈpɔːtɪŋ/ ________

semi- /ˈsemi/ ________

set up ⊸ /ˌset ˈʌp/ ________

shortage /ˈʃɔːtɪdʒ/ ________

slow down ⊸ /ˌsləʊ ˈdaʊn/ ________

smart ⊸ /smɑːt/ ________

software ⊸ /ˈsɒftweə(r)/ ________

solar power /ˌsəʊlə ˈpaʊə(r)/ ________

sonic /ˈsɒnɪk/ ________

source ⊸ /sɔːs/ ________

space exploration /ˈspeɪs ekspləˌreɪʃn/ ________

space race ⊸ /ˈspeɪs ˌreɪs/ ________

spontaneously /spɒnˈteɪniəsli/ ________

state of the art ⊸ /ˈsteɪt əv ði ˌɑːt/ ________

sub- /sʌb/ ________

target ⊸ /ˈtɑːgɪt/ ________

the best way to ⊸ /ðə ˈbest ˌweɪ tə/ ________

think for yourself ⊸ /ˌθɪŋk fə jɔːˈself/ ________

treat ⊸ /triːt/ ________

twenty years from now ⊸ /ˈtwenti ˌjɪəz frəm ˌnaʊ/ ________

ultimate ⊸ /ˈʌltɪmət/ ________

unconventional /ʌnkənˈvenʃənl/ ________

uninhabitable /ʌnɪnˈhæbɪtəbl/ ________

username /ˈjuːzəneɪm/ ________

vision of ⊸ /ˈvɪʒn əv/ ________

wacky /ˈwæki/ ________

website ⊸ /ˈwebsaɪt/ ________

what is more ... ⊸ /ˌwɒt ɪz ˈmɔː(r)/ ________

Additional vocabulary

/p/ **p**en	/d/ **d**og	/tʃ/ bea**ch**	/v/ **v**ery	/s/ **s**peak	/ʒ/ televi**s**ion	/n/ **n**ow	/r/ **r**adio
/b/ **b**ig	/k/ **c**an	/dʒ/ **j**ob	/θ/ **th**ink	/z/ **z**oo	/h/ **h**ouse	/ŋ/ si**ng**	/j/ **y**es
/t/ **t**wo	/g/ **g**ood	/f/ **f**ood	/ð/ **th**en	/ʃ/ **sh**e	/m/ **m**eat	/l/ **l**ate	/w/ **w**e

acquit sb /ə'kwɪt/
allege /ə'ledʒ/
announce /ə'naʊns/
appear in court /əˌpɪər ɪn 'kɔːt/
apron /'eɪprən/
argue /'ɑːgjuː/
armchair /'ɑːmtʃeə(r)/
balance /'bæləns/
balcony /'bælkəni/
basin /'beɪsn/
bear /beə(r)/
believe in sth (phr v) /bɪ'liːv ˌɪn/
bookcase /'bʊkkeɪs/
butcher /'bʊtʃə(r)/
carpet /'kɑːpɪt/
charge sb with a crime /ˌtʃɑːdʒ ˌ... wɪð ə 'kraɪm/
chest of drawers /ˌtʃest əv 'drɔːz/
claim /kleɪm/
coffin /'kɒfɪn/
confess /kən'fes/
convince /kən'vɪns/
cooker /'kʊkə(r)/
corroborate /kə'rɒbəreɪt/
court case /'kɔːt ˌkeɪs/
creature /'kriːtʃə(r)/
cupboard /'kʌbəd/
curtain /'kɜːtn/
deceased (adj) /dɪ'siːst/
defend /dɪ'fend/
dining table /'daɪnɪŋ ˌteɪbl/
disagreeable /dɪsə'griːəbl/
dishonest /dɪs'ɒnɪst/
disorganized /dɪs'ɔːgənaɪzd/
dissatisfied /dɪs'sætɪsfaɪd/
drainpipe /'dreɪnpaɪp/
drown /draʊn/
enquire /ɪŋ'kwaɪə(r)/
fake /feɪk/
find sb (not) guilty /faɪnd ... (ˌnɒt) 'gɪlti/
fireplace /'faɪəpleɪs/
flower bed /'flaʊə ˌbed/
fluently /'fluːəntli/
footprint /'fʊtprɪnt/
give evidence /ˌgɪv 'evɪdəns/
groan /grəʊn/
guilty /'gɪlti/
hear evidence /ˌhɪər 'evɪdəns/
hedge /hedʒ/
heir (n) /eə(r)/
here and now /ˌhɪər ən 'naʊ/
hire /'haɪə(r)/
hoax /həʊks/
homeless /'həʊmləs/
home-made /ˌhəʊm 'meɪd/
homesick /'həʊmsɪk/
homeward /'həʊmwəd/
hound (n) /haʊnd/
housebound /'haʊsbaʊnd/
household /'haʊshəʊld/
housekeeper /'haʊskiːpə(r)/
house-proud /'haʊspraʊd/
illegal /ɪ'liːgl/
illegible /ɪ'ledʒəbl/
illiterate /ɪ'lɪtərət/
illogical /ɪ'lɒdʒɪkl/
impatient /ɪm'peɪʃnt/
impossible /ɪm'pɒsəbl/
impostor /ɪm'pɒstə(r)/
impractical /ɪm'præktɪkl/
in spite of /ɪn 'spaɪt əv/
indecisive /ɪndɪ'saɪsɪv/
inform (v) /ɪn'fɔːm/
informal /ɪn'fɔːml/
insensitive /ɪn'sensətɪv/
invest /ɪn'vest/
invisible /ɪn'vɪzəbl/
irrational /ɪ'ræʃnəl/

/i/ happy	/æ/ flag	/ɜː/ her	/ʊ/ look	/ʌ/ mum	/ɔɪ/ noisy	/ɪə/ here
/ɪ/ it	/ɑː/ art	/ɒ/ not	/uː/ you	/eɪ/ day	/aʊ/ how	/eə/ wear
/iː/ he	/e/ egg	/ɔː/ four	/ə/ sugar	/aɪ/ why	/əʊ/ go	/ʊə/ tourist

irregular /ɪ'regjələ(r)/ ______
irrelevant /ɪ'reləvənt/ ______
irresponsible /ɪrɪ'spɒnsəbl/ ______
judge 🔑 /dʒʌdʒ/ ______
jury /'dʒʊəri/ ______
ladle /'leɪdl/ ______
lawn /lɔːn/ ______
make a reservation 🔑 /ˌmeɪk ə rezə'veɪʃn/ ______
mantelpiece /'mæntlpiːs/ ______
mature /mə'tʃʊə(r)/ ______
mirror 🔑 /'mɪrə(r)/ ______
mutter /'mʌtə(r)/ ______
overjoyed /əʊvə'dʒɔɪd/ ______
path 🔑 /pɑːθ/ ______
payable /'peɪəbl/ ______
plead (not) guilty /ˌpliːd (ˌnɒt) 'gɪlti/ ______
poverty /'pɒvəti/ ______
precious /'preʃəs/ ______
presumed /prɪ'zjuːmd/ ______
prove 🔑 /pruːv/ ______
reach a verdict /ˌriːtʃ ə 'vɜːdɪkt/ ______
refuse to do sth 🔑 /rɪˌfjuːz tə 'duː/ ______
represent 🔑 /reprɪ'zent/ ______
respond 🔑 /rɪ'spɒnd/ ______
rug /rʌg/ ______
saucepan /'sɔːspən/ ______
scream 🔑 /skriːm/ ______
send sb to prison 🔑 /ˌsend ... tə 'prɪzn/ ______
sentence 🔑 /'sentəns/ ______
shears /ʃɪəz/ ______
sighting 🔑 /'saɪtɪŋ/ ______
sink 🔑 /sɪŋk/ ______
sofa /'səʊfə/ ______
spend the night 🔑 /ˌspend ðə 'naɪt/ ______
stepladder /'steplædə(r)/ ______
stool /stuːl/ ______
stove 🔑 /stəʊv/ ______

the accused 🔑 /ðiː ə'kjuːzd/ ______
the defence 🔑 /ðə dɪ'fens/ ______
the prosecution /ðə prɒsɪ'kjuːʃn/ ______
there and then 🔑 /ˌðeər ən 'ðen/ ______
trial 🔑 /'traɪəl/ ______
unstable /ʌn'steɪbl/ ______
untidy 🔑 /ʌn'taɪdi/ ______
vase /vɑːz/ ______
wardrobe /'wɔːdrəʊb/ ______
webcam /'webkæm/ ______
whisper 🔑 /'wɪspə(r)/ ______
witness 🔑 /'wɪtnəs/ ______
Would you mind ...? 🔑 /ˌwʊd juː 'maɪnd/ ______
yell 🔑 /jel/ ______

Additional vocabulary

/p/ **p**en	/d/ **d**og	/tʃ/ **be**a**ch**	/v/ **v**ery	/s/ **s**peak	/ʒ/ televi**si**on	/n/ **n**ow	/r/ **r**adio
/b/ **b**ig	/k/ **c**an	/dʒ/ **j**ob	/θ/ **th**ink	/z/ **z**oo	/h/ **h**ouse	/ŋ/ si**ng**	/j/ **y**es
/t/ **t**wo	/g/ **g**ood	/f/ **f**ood	/ð/ **th**en	/ʃ/ **sh**e	/m/ **m**eat	/l/ **l**ate	/w/ **w**e

a shoulder to cry on /ə ˌʃəʊldə tə 'kraɪ ˌɒn/

accept my apologies for /əkˌsept maɪ ə'pɒlədʒiz/

accept responsibility for /əkˌsept rɪsponsə'bɪləti fə/

acquaintance /ə'kweɪntəns/

admire /əd'maɪə(r)/

admit responsibility /ədˌmɪt rɪspɒnsə'bɪləti/

advice line /əd'vaɪs ˌlaɪn/

after all /ˌɑːftər 'ɔːl/

amused /ə'mjuːzd/

amusing /ə'mjuːzɪŋ/

annoyed /ə'nɔɪd/

annoying /ə'nɔɪɪŋ/

apologize for /ə'pɒlədʒaɪz fə(r)/

at heart /ət 'hɑːt/

back sb up in an argument /ˌbæk ... ˌʌp ɪn ən 'ɑːgjumənt/

beyond /bɪ'jɒnd/

boss /bɒs/

bottom of my heart /ˌbɒtəm əv ˌmaɪ 'hɑːt/

by heart /ˌbaɪ 'hɑːt/

catch a glimpse of /'kætʃ ə ˌglɪmps əv/

change of heart /ˌtʃeɪndʒ əv 'hɑːt/

classmate /'klɑːsmeɪt/

close to my heart /ˌkləʊs tə ˌmaɪ 'hɑːt/

colleague /'kɒliːg/

come up with sth /ˌkʌm 'ʌp ˌwɪð/

concern /kən'sɜːn/

confide in sb /kən'faɪd ɪn .../

crisis /'kraɪsɪs/

cut down on sth /ˌkʌt 'daʊn ˌɒn .../

depressed /dɪ'prest/

depressing /dɪ'presɪŋ/

effective /ɪ'fektɪv/

entertaining /entə'teɪnɪŋ/

exhausted /ɪg'zɔːstɪd/

exhausting /ɪg'zɔːstɪŋ/

fall out with sb /ˌfɔːl 'aʊt wɪð/

fascinated /'fæsɪneɪtɪd/

fascinating /'fæsɪneɪtɪŋ/

financial help /faɪˌnænʃl, fə'næ- 'help/

find out about /ˌfaɪnd 'aʊt əˌbaʊt/

formal apology /ˌfɔːml ə'pɒlədʒi/

frightened /'fraɪtnd/

frightening /'fraɪtnɪŋ/

genuine /'dʒenjuɪn/

get away with sth /ˌget ə'weɪ wɪð/

get on (well) with sb /ˌget ˌɒn ('wel) wɪð/

glimpse /glɪmps/

group holiday /ˌgruːp 'hɒlədeɪ/

hang out with sb /ˌhæŋ 'aʊt wɪd/

heart and soul /ˌhɑːt ənd 'səʊl/

heart of gold /ˌhɑːt əv 'gəʊld/

in common /ˌɪn 'kɒmən/

in the end /ˌɪn ði 'end/

incident /'ɪnsɪdənt/

interrupt /ɪntə'rʌpt/

isolated /'aɪsəleɪtɪd/

it really gets me down /ɪt ˌrɪːəli ˌgets miː 'daʊn/

judge /dʒʌdʒ/

keep in touch with sb /ˌkiːp ˌɪn 'tʌtʃ wɪð/

lend sb a hand /ˌlend ... ə 'hænd/

let sb down /ˌlet ... 'daʊn/

lifetime /'laɪftaɪm/

/i/ happy	/æ/ flag	/ɜː/ her	/ʊ/ look	/ʌ/ mum	/ɔɪ/ noisy	/ɪə/ here
/ɪ/ it	/ɑː/ art	/ɒ/ not	/uː/ you	/eɪ/ day	/aʊ/ how	/eə/ wear
/iː/ he	/e/ egg	/ɔː/ four	/ə/ sugar	/aɪ/ why	/əʊ/ go	/ʊə/ tourist

look down on sb 🔑 /ˌlʊk ˈdaʊn ˌɒn/ ______

look forward to sth 🔑 /ˌlʊk ˈfɔːwəd tə/ ______

look up to sb 🔑 /ˌlʊk ˈʌp tə/ ______

lose touch with sb 🔑 /ˌluːz ˈtʌtʃ wɪð/ ______

magazine survey 🔑 /mæɡəˈziːn ˌsɜːveɪ/ ______

make friends with 🔑 /ˌmeɪk ˈfrendz wɪð/ ______

make up after an argument 🔑 /ˌmeɪk ˌʌp ˌɑːftər ən ˈɑːɡjumənt/ ______

modern life 🔑 /ˌmɒdn ˈlaɪf/ ______

obligation /ɒblɪˈɡeɪʃn/ ______

on the go 🔑 /ˌɒn ðə ˈɡəʊ/ ______

otherwise 🔑 /ˈʌðəwaɪz/ ______

outfit /ˈaʊtfɪt/ ______

penfriend /ˈpenfrend/ ______

Personally, ... 🔑 /ˈpɜːsənəli/ ______

put up with sth/sb 🔑 /ˌpʊt ˈʌp wɪð/ ______

regard 🔑 /rɪˈɡɑːd/ ______

registered 🔑 /ˈredʒɪstəd/ ______

regret 🔑 /rɪˈɡret/ ______

relative 🔑 /ˈrelətɪv/ ______

resounding /rɪˈzaʊndɪŋ/ ______

run out of sth 🔑 /ˌrʌn ˈaʊt əv/ ______

satisfied 🔑 /ˈsætɪsfaɪd/ ______

satisfying 🔑 /ˈsætɪsfaɪɪŋ/ ______

saunter /ˈsɔːntə(r)/ ______

sibling /ˈsɪblɪŋ/ ______

social activity 🔑 /ˌsəʊʃl ækˈtɪvəti/ ______

social circle 🔑 /ˌsəʊʃl ˈsɜːkl/ ______

spouse /spaʊs/ ______

stand up for sb 🔑 /ˌstænd ˈʌp fə/ ______

That depends 🔑 /ˌðæt dɪˈpendz/ ______

to heart 🔑 /tə ˈhɑːt/ ______

tolerate /ˈtɒləreɪt/ ______

treat 🔑 /triːt/ ______

tropical island 🔑 /ˌtrɒpɪkl ˈaɪlənd/ ______

true friend 🔑 /ˌtruː ˈfrend/ ______

unselfish /ʌnˈselfɪʃ/ ______

wheelchair /ˈwiːltʃeə(r)/ ______

work freelance /ˌwɜːk ˈfriːlɑːns/ ______

Additional vocabulary

/p/ **p**en	/d/ **d**og	/tʃ/ bea**ch**	/v/ **v**ery	/s/ **s**peak	/ʒ/ televi**si**on	/n/ **n**ow	/r/ **r**adio
/b/ **b**ig	/k/ **c**an	/dʒ/ **j**ob	/θ/ **th**ink	/z/ **z**oo	/h/ **h**ouse	/ŋ/ si**ng**	/j/ **y**es
/t/ **t**wo	/ɡ/ **g**ood	/f/ **f**ood	/ð/ **th**en	/ʃ/ **sh**e	/m/ **m**eat	/l/ **l**ate	/w/ **w**e

abandon /ə'bændən/
absolute /'æbsəluːt/
affordable /ə'fɔːdəbl/
air traffic controller /ˌeə ˌtræfɪk kən'trəʊlə(r)/
arrive at /ə'raɪv ət/
awesome /'ɔːsəm/
baggage reclaim /'bægɪdʒ ˌriːkleɪm/
be the first to ... /ˌbi ðə 'fɜːst tə/
boast /bəʊst/
break into /breɪk/
budget airline /ˌbʌdʒɪt 'eəlaɪn/
cab /kæb/
camping holiday /'kæmpɪŋ ˌhɒlədeɪ/
care /keə(r)/
carriage /'kærɪdʒ/
ceiling (n) /'siːlɪŋ/
change /tʃeɪndʒ/
cheap /tʃiːp/
city break /ˌsɪti 'breɪk/
complain about /kəm'pleɪn/
convenient /kən'viːniənt/
cross /krɒs/
crossing /'krɒsɪŋ/
cruise /kruːz/
customs /'kʌstəmz/
dangerous /'deɪndʒərəs/
dart /dɑːt/
day trip /'deɪ ˌtrɪp/
delay /dɪ'leɪ/
departure lounge /dɪ'pɑːtʃə(r)/
departures board /dɪ'pɑːtʃəz ˌbɔːd/
dream holiday /ˌdriːm 'hɒlədeɪ/
dream of /driːm/
economical /iːkə'nɒmɪkl/
environmentally-friendly /ɪnvaɪrənˌmentəli 'frendli/
escalator /'eskəleɪtə(r)/
excursion /ɪk'skɜːʃn/
expedition /ekspə'dɪʃn/
expensive /ɪk'spensɪv/
face-to-face /ˌfeɪs tə 'feɪs/
fatal /'feɪtl/
flight /flaɪt/
grow in popularity /ˌgrəʊ ɪn pɒpjə'lærəti/
hard to find /ˌhɑːd tə 'faɪnd/
have a terrible time /ˌhæv ə 'terəbl ˌtaɪm/
healthy /'helθi/
hobble /'hɒbl/
holiday destination /'hɒlədeɪ destɪˌneɪʃn/
holiday makers /'hɒlədeɪ ˌmeɪkəz/
hurtle /'hɜːtl/
impact /'ɪmpækt/
jump /dʒʌmp/
land /lænd/
lazy (adj) /'leɪzi/
limp /lɪmp/
listen to /'lɪsn ˌtuː, tə/
lock (v) /lɒk/
long-haul flight /ˌlɒŋ ˌhɔːl 'flaɪt/
look at /'lʊk ˌæt, ət/
luggage rack /'lʌgɪdʒ ˌræk/
marking /'mɑːkɪŋ/
mass-produce /ˌmæs prə'djuːs/
mud hut /ˌmʌd 'hʌt/
nocturnal /nɒk'tɜːnl/
pace /peɪs/
package holiday /'pækɪdʒ ˌhɒlədeɪ/
passport control /ˌpɑːspɔːt kən'trəʊl/
plain /pleɪn/
platform /'plætfɔːm/
pop sth into sth /'pɒp ... ˌɪntə .../

/i/ happy	/æ/ flag	/ɜː/ her	/ʊ/ look	/ʌ/ mum	/ɔɪ/ noisy	/ɪə/ here
/ɪ/ it	/ɑː/ art	/ɒ/ not	/uː/ you	/eɪ/ day	/aʊ/ how	/eə/ wear
/iː/ he	/e/ egg	/ɔː/ four	/ə/ sugar	/aɪ/ why	/əʊ/ go	/ʊə/ tourist

recent (adj) /ˈriːsnt/
relaxing /rɪˈlæksɪŋ/
reliable /rɪˈlaɪəbl/
round-the-world trip /ˌraʊnd ðə ˌwɜːld ˈtrɪp/
rucksack /ˈrʌksæk/
runway /ˈrʌnweɪ/
ski resort /ˈskiː rɪˌzɔːt/
slash /slæʃ/
slow /sləʊ/
soaked /səʊkt/
spot /spɒt/
spring /sprɪŋ/
stare /steə(r)/
stealthy /ˈstelθi/
stressful /ˈstresfl/
stride /straɪd/
stroll /strəʊl/
struggle to survive /ˌstrʌgl tə səˈvaɪv/
suffer a setback /ˌsʌfər ə ˈsetbæk/
suicide note /ˈsuːɪsaɪd ˌnəʊt/
take to the air /ˌteɪk tə ði ˈeə(r)/
tear (after sb/sth) /ˌteər ˈɑːftə(r)/
the side of the road /ðə ˌsaɪd əv ðə ˈrəʊd/
thump /θʌmp/
tour /tʊə(r)/
track /træk/
traffic jam /ˈtræfɪk ˌdʒæm/
trail /treɪl/
travel /ˈtrævl/
trip /trɪp/
trolley /ˈtrɒli/
trudge /trʌdʒ/
trundle /ˈtrʌndl/
trunk /trʌŋk/
unbelievably /ʌnbɪˈliːvəbli/
uncomfortable /ʌnˈkʌmftəbl/
unreliable /ʌnrɪˈlaɪəbl/
up /ʌp/
waiting room /ˈweɪtɪŋ ˌruːm/
winter sports /ˌwɪntə ˈspɔːts/

Additional vocabulary

/p/ **p**en	/d/ **d**og	/tʃ/ bea**ch**	/v/ **v**ery	/s/ **s**peak	/ʒ/ televi**si**on	/n/ **n**ow	/r/ **r**adio
/b/ **b**ig	/k/ **c**an	/dʒ/ **j**ob	/θ/ **th**ink	/z/ **z**oo	/h/ **h**ouse	/ŋ/ si**ng**	/j/ **y**es
/t/ **t**wo	/g/ **g**ood	/f/ **f**ood	/ð/ **th**en	/ʃ/ **sh**e	/m/ **m**eat	/l/ **l**ate	/w/ **w**e

ask for a loan ⊶ /ˌɑːsk fər ə ˈləʊn/ ______
at (his) own expense ⊶ /ət … ˌəʊn ɪkspens/ ______
at first sight ⊶ /ət ˌfɜːst ˈsaɪt/ ______
auction /ˈɔːkʃn/ ______
ball gown /ˈbɔːl ˌgaʊn/ ______
bargain ⊶ /ˈbɑːgɪn/ ______
be able to afford sth ⊶ /ˌbiː ˌeɪbl tu əˈfɔːd/ ______
be in the red ⊶ /ˌbiː ɪn ðə ˈred/ ______
boom /buːm/ ______
break into ⊶ /ˈbreɪk ˌɪntə/ ______
by chance ⊶ /ˌbaɪ ˈtʃɑːns/ ______
by mistake ⊶ /ˌbaɪ mɪˈsteɪk/ ______
can't make ends meet ⊶ /ˌkɑːnt ˌmeɪk ˌendz ˈmiːt/ ______
cash machine ⊶ /ˈkæʃ məˌʃiːn/ ______
change money ⊶ /ˌtʃeɪndʒ ˈmʌni/ ______
cheque ⊶ /tʃek/ ______
come across ⊶ /ˈkʌm əˌkrɒs/ ______
conversion /kənˈvɜːʃn/ ______
cost a fortune ⊶ /ˌkɒst ə ˈfɔːtʃuːn/ ______
count on sb ⊶ /ˈkaʊnt ˌɒn/ ______
credit card ⊶ /ˈkredɪt ˌkɑːd/ ______
currency /ˈkʌrənsi/ ______
current account ⊶ /ˌkʌrənt əˈkaʊnt/ ______
debit card /ˈdebɪt ˌkɑːd/ ______
do sth on a regular basis ⊶ /ˌduː … ˌɒn ə ˌregjələ ˈbeɪsɪs/ ______
do without sth ⊶ /ˌduː wɪˈðaʊt/ ______
donate /dəʊˈneɪt/ ______
draughty /ˈdrɑːfti/ ______
driveway /ˈdraɪvweɪ/ ______
emigrate ⊶ /ˈemɪgreɪt/ ______
entire ⊶ /ɪnˈtaɪə(r)/ ______
entrepreneur /ɒntrəprəˈnɜː(r)/ ______
exceed /ɪkˈsiːd/ ______
exchange rate /ɪksˈtʃeɪndʒ ˌreɪt/ ______
for a change ⊶ /ˌfər ə ˈtʃeɪndʒ/ ______
for fun ⊶ /fə ˈfʌn/ ______
from bad to worse ⊶ /frəm ˌbæd tə ˈwɜːs/ ______
from scratch ⊶ /frəm ˈskrætʃ/ ______
gift ⊶ /gɪft/ ______
give sth away ⊶ /ˌgɪv … əˈweɪ/ ______
go over ⊶ /ˌgəʊ ˈəʊvə(r)/ ______
go with sth ⊶ /ˈgəʊ ˌwɪð/ ______
goal ⊶ /gəʊl/ ______
hard up ⊶ /ˌhɑːd ˈʌp/ ______
head above water ⊶ /ˌhed əˌbʌv ˈwɔːtə(r)/ ______
host ⊶ /həʊst/ ______
housing market ⊶ /ˈhaʊzɪŋ ˌmɑːkɪt/ ______
immigrant /ˈɪmɪgrənt/ ______
in debt ⊶ /ɪn ˈdet/ ______
invest ⊶ /ɪnˈvest/ ______
junk dealer /ˈdʒʌŋk ˌdiːlə(r)/ ______
leave everything to the last minute ⊶ /ˌliːv ˌevriθɪŋ tə ðə ˌlɑːst ˈmɪnɪt/ ______
look after ⊶ /ˌlʊk ˈɑːftə(r)/ ______
look back on (your life) ⊶ /ˌlʊk ˈbæk ɒn (jɔː ˌlaɪf)/ ______
make a fortune ⊶ /ˌmeɪk ə ˈfɔːtʃuːn/ ______
manufacture ⊶ /mænjuˈfæktʃə(r)/ ______
match ⊶ /mætʃ/ ______
medical research ⊶ /ˌmedɪkl rɪˈsɜːtʃ, ˈriːsɜːtʃ/ ______

/i/ **happy**	/æ/ **flag**	/ɜː/ **her**	/ʊ/ **look**	/ʌ/ **mum**	/ɔɪ/ **noisy**	/ɪə/ **here**
/ɪ/ **it**	/ɑː/ **art**	/ɒ/ **not**	/uː/ **you**	/eɪ/ **day**	/aʊ/ **how**	/eə/ **wear**
/iː/ **he**	/e/ **egg**	/ɔː/ **four**	/ə/ **sugar**	/aɪ/ **why**	/əʊ/ **go**	/ʊə/ **tourist**

money can't buy you happiness ⊶ /ˌmʌni ˌkɑːnt ˌbaɪ juː ˈhæpɪnəs/

newspaper column ⊶ /ˈnjuːzpeɪpə ˌkɒləm/

nobody in their right mind would ... ⊶ /ˈnəʊbədi ɪn ðeə ˌraɪt ˌmaɪnd ˌwʊd .../

note ⊶ /nəʊt/

on a regular basis ⊶ /ˌɒn ə ˌregjələ ˈbeɪsɪs/

on the ball ⊶ /ˌɒn ðə ˈbɔːl/

on the contrary /ˌɒn ðə ˈkɒntrəri/

on the go ⊶ /ˌɒn ðə ˈgəʊ/

on the way to ⊶ /ˌɒn ðə ˈweɪ tə/

out of touch ⊶ /ˌaʊt əv ˈtʌtʃ/

out of work ⊶ /ˌaʊt əv ˈwɜːk/

overcharge for sth /əʊvəˈtʃɑːdʒ fə .../

pannier /ˈpæniə(r)/

pass away ⊶ /ˌpɑːs əˈweɪ/

pay by credit card ⊶ /ˌpeɪ ˌbaɪ ˈkredɪt ˌkɑːd/

pay for sth in cash ⊶ /ˌpeɪ fə ... ɪn ˈkæʃ/

pick on ⊶ /ˈpɪk ˌɒn/

PIN /pɪn/

pocket money ⊶ /ˈpɒkɪt ˌmʌni/

range ⊶ /reɪndʒ/

rate of interest ⊶ /ˌreɪt əv ˈɪntrəst/

receipt ⊶ /rɪˈsiːt/

refugee /refjuˈdʒiː/

regret ⊶ /rɪˈgret/

risky /ˈrɪski/

rolling in money ⊶ /ˈrəʊlɪŋ ɪn ˌmʌni/

rough terrain /ˌrʌf təˈreɪn/

save up ⊶ /ˌseɪv ˈʌp/

savings account ⊶ /ˈseɪvɪŋz əˌkaʊnt/

settle ⊶ /ˈsetl/

spend money ⊶ /ˌspend ˈmʌni/

surely ⊶ /ˈʃʊəli/

take money out of sth ⊶ /ˌteɪk ˈmʌni ˌaʊt/

talent /ˈtælənt/

thanks a million ⊶ /ˌθæŋks ə ˈmɪljən/

the great outdoors ⊶ /ðə ˌgreɪt aʊtˈdɔːz/

tighten (our) belt(s) /ˌtaɪtn ... ˈbelt(s)/

under (her) breath ⊶ /ˌʌndə ... ˈbreθ/

under control ⊶ /ˌʌndə kənˈtrəʊl/

vast ⊶ /vɑːst/

venture ⊶ /ˈventʃə(r)/

waste money ⊶ /ˌweɪst ˈmʌni/

worth every penny ⊶ /ˌwɜːθ ˌevri ˈpeni/

write to enquire about /ˈraɪt tu ɪnˌkwaɪər əˌbaʊt/

Additional vocabulary

/p/ pen	/d/ dog	/tʃ/ beach	/v/ very	/s/ speak	/ʒ/ television	/n/ now	/r/ radio
/b/ big	/k/ can	/dʒ/ job	/θ/ think	/z/ zoo	/h/ house	/ŋ/ sing	/j/ yes
/t/ two	/g/ good	/f/ food	/ð/ then	/ʃ/ she	/m/ meat	/l/ late	/w/ we

abstract art /ˌæbstrækt 'ɑːt/ ______

abstract painting /'æbstrækt ˌpeɪntɪŋ/ ______

accompany 🔑 /ə'kʌmpəni/ ______

angle 🔑 /'æŋgl/ ______

apart from 🔑 /ə'pɑːt frəm/ ______

aria /'ɑːriə/ ______

arrogant /'ærəgənt/ ______

audience 🔑 /'ɔːdiəns/ ______

be in trouble with 🔑 /ˌbiː ɪn 'trʌbl ˌwɪð/ ______

be made up (of) 🔑 /ˌbi 'meɪd ˌʌp (əv)/ ______

be regarded as 🔑 /ˌbi rɪ'gɑːdɪd əz/ ______

big business 🔑 /ˌbɪg 'bɪznəs/ ______

billboard /'bɪlbɔːd/ ______

blow (your) own trumpet /ˌbləʊ ... ˌəʊn 'trʌmpɪt/ ______

brickwork /'brɪkwɜːk/ ______

busker /'bʌskə(r)/ ______

cave /keɪv/ ______

change into a costume /ˌtʃeɪndʒ ˌɪntu ə 'kɒstjuːm/ ______

change (your) tune 🔑 /ˌtʃeɪndʒ ... 'tjuːn/ ______

charge sb to do sth 🔑 /ˌtʃɑːdʒ ... tə 'duː .../ ______

charity 🔑 /'tʃærəti/ ______

claim 🔑 /kleɪm/ ______

cold-hearted (adj) /ˌkəʊld 'hɑːtɪd/ ______

composer /kəm'pəʊzə(r)/ ______

conductor /kən'dʌktə(r)/ ______

consumer 🔑 /'kənsjuːmə(r)/ ______

contain some comment about 🔑 /kən'teɪn ˌsʌm ˌkɒment əˌbaʊt/ ______

convincing 🔑 /kən'vɪnsɪŋ/ ______

depict /dɪ'pɪkt/ ______

director 🔑 /də'rektə(r), dɪ-, daɪ-/ ______

disadvantaged 🔑 /dɪsəd'vɑːntɪdʒd/ ______

discard /dɪs'kɑːd/ ______

drum kit /'drʌm ˌkɪt/ ______

elaborate /ɪ'læbərət/ ______

extensive 🔑 /ɪk'stensɪv/ ______

face the music 🔑 /ˌfeɪs ðə 'mjuːzɪk/ ______

factor 🔑 /'fæktə(r)/ ______

financial 🔑 /faɪ'nænʃl, fə'næ-/ ______

from a certain angle 🔑 /frəm ə 'sɜːtn ˌæŋgl/ ______

gig /gɪg/ ______

give an impression of 🔑 /ˌgɪv ən ɪm'preʃn əv/ ______

graceful /'greɪsfl/ ______

graffiti /grə'fiːti/ ______

have sth down to a fine art 🔑 /ˌhæv ... ˌdaʊn tu ə ˌfaɪn 'ɑːt/ ______

hopeless /'həʊpləs/ ______

household name 🔑 /ˌhaʊshəʊld 'neɪm/ ______

in the foreground /ˌɪn ðə 'fɔːgraʊnd/ ______

incorporate into /ɪn'kɔːpəreɪt ˌɪntə/ ______

inherit /ɪn'herɪt/ ______

inheritance /ɪn'herɪtəns/ ______

instrument 🔑 /'ɪnstrəmənt/ ______

intend 🔑 /ɪn'tend/ ______

juggling /'dʒʌglɪŋ/ ______

keep sth a secret 🔑 /ˌkiːp ... ə 'siːkrət/ ______

kind 🔑 /kaɪnd/ ______

landscape 🔑 /'lændskeɪp/ ______

lighting 🔑 /'laɪtɪŋ/ ______

lines 🔑 /laɪnz/ ______

lyrics /'lɪrɪks/ ______

make a song and dance about sth 🔑 /ˌmeɪk ə ˌsɒŋ ən 'dɑːns əˌbaʊt .../ ______

melody /'melədi/ ______

mike /maɪk/ ______

mysterious 🔑 /mɪ'stɪəriəs/ ______

novel 🔑 /'nɒvl/ ______

/i/ happy	/æ/ flag	/ɜː/ her	/ʊ/ look	/ʌ/ mum	/ɔɪ/ noisy	/ɪə/ here
/ɪ/ it	/ɑː/ art	/ɒ/ not	/uː/ you	/eɪ/ day	/aʊ/ how	/eə/ wear
/iː/ he	/e/ egg	/ɔː/ four	/ə/ sugar	/aɪ/ why	/əʊ/ go	/ʊə/ tourist

novelist /ˈnɒvəlɪst/ ___
overweight /əʊvəˈweɪt/ ___
peaceful 🔑 /ˈpiːsfl/ ___
pedestrian /pəˈdestriən/ ___
performance art 🔑 /pəˌfɔːməns ˈɑːt/ ___
performing arts 🔑 /pəˌfɔːmɪŋ ˈɑːts/ ___
pester power /ˈpestə ˌpaʊə(r)/ ___
play 🔑 /pleɪ/ ___
playwright /ˈpleɪraɪt/ ___
pleasurable /ˈpleʒərəbl/ ___
poet /ˈpəʊɪt/ ___
poetic /pəʊˈetɪk/ ___
portable /ˈpɔːtəbl/ ___
portrait /ˈpɔːtreɪt/ ___
pothole /ˈpɒthəʊl/ ___
prepare sb for sth 🔑 /prɪˈpeə ˌ... fə/ ___
primitive /ˈprɪmətɪv/ ___
publicity stunt /pʌbˈlɪsəti ˌstʌnt/ ___
put sb in the picture 🔑 /ˌpʊt ... ɪn ðə ˈpɪktʃə(r)/ ___
read sb like a book 🔑 /ˌriːd ... ˌlaɪk ə ˈbʊk/ ___
recital /rɪˈsaɪtl/ ___
rehearse a scene /rɪˌhɜːs ə ˈsiːn/ ___
role 🔑 /rəʊl/ ___
screenplay /ˈskriːnpleɪ/ ___
script /skrɪpt/ ___
scriptwriter /ˈskrɪptraɪtə(r)/ ___
sculptor /ˈskʌlptə(r)/ ___
sculpture /ˈskʌlptʃə(r)/ ___
selfish (adj) /ˈselfɪʃ/ ___
shower 🔑 /ˈʃaʊə(r)/ ___
sketch /sketʃ/ ___
songwriter /ˈsɒŋraɪtə(r)/ ___
stage hand 🔑 /ˈsteɪdʒ ˌhænd/ ___
stage musical 🔑 /ˌsteɪdʒ ˈmjuːzɪkl/ ___
startle /ˈstɑːtl/ ___
steal the show 🔑 /ˌstiːl ðə ˈʃəʊ/ ___
still life 🔑 /ˌstɪl ˈlaɪf/ ___
striking 🔑 /ˈstraɪkɪŋ/ ___
subject matter 🔑 /ˈsʌbdʒɪkt ˌmætə(r)/ ___
sum up 🔑 /ˌsʌm ˈʌp/ ___
surface 🔑 /ˈsɜːfɪs/ ___
survive 🔑 (v) /səˈvaɪv/ ___
swerve /swɜːv/ ___
symphony /ˈsɪmfəni/ ___
thoughtfully /ˈθɔːtfəli/ ___
urban 🔑 /ˈɜːbən/ ___
vending machine /ˈvendɪŋ məˌʃiːn/ ___
visual arts /ˌvɪʒuəl ˈɑːts/ ___
voucher /ˈvaʊtʃə(r)/ ___
wooden 🔑 /ˈwʊdn/ ___

Additional vocabulary

/p/ **p**en	/d/ **d**og	/tʃ/ bea**ch**	/v/ **v**ery	/s/ **s**peak	/ʒ/ televi**s**ion	/n/ **n**ow	/r/ **r**adio
/b/ **b**ig	/k/ **c**an	/dʒ/ **j**ob	/θ/ **th**ink	/z/ **z**oo	/h/ **h**ouse	/ŋ/ si**ng**	/j/ **y**es
/t/ **t**wo	/g/ **g**ood	/f/ **f**ood	/ð/ **th**en	/ʃ/ **sh**e	/m/ **m**eat	/l/ **l**ate	/w/ **w**e

IRREGULAR VERBS

Base form	Past simple	Past participle
be	was/were	been
bear	bore	borne
become	became	become
begin	began	begun
bend	bent	bent
bite	bit	bitten
blow	blew	blown
break	broke	broken
bring	brought	brought
build	built	built
burn	burnt	burnt
buy	bought	bought
can	could	been able to
catch	caught	caught
choose	chose	chosen
come	came	come
cost	cost	cost
cut	cut	cut
deal	dealt	dealt
do	did	done
draw	drew	drawn
drink	drank	drunk
drive	drove	driven
eat	ate	eaten
fall	fell	fallen
feed	fed	fed
feel	felt	felt
fight	fought	fought
find	found	found
fly	flew	flown
forget	forgot	forgotten
get	got	got
give	gave	given
go	went	gone/been
grow	grew	grown
hang	hung	hung
have	had	had
hear	heard	heard
hide	hid	hidden
hit	hit	hit
hold	held	held
keep	kept	kept
know	knew	known
lay	laid	laid
lead	led	led
learn	learnt/-ed	learnt/-ed
leave	left	left
lend	lent	lent
lose	lost	lost

Base form	Past simple	Past participle
make	made	made
mean	meant	meant
meet	met	met
overcome	overcame	overcome
pay	paid	paid
put	put	put
read	read	read
ride	rode	ridden
ring	rang	rung
run	ran	run
say	said	said
see	saw	seen
sell	sold	sold
send	sent	sent
set	set	set
shake	shook	shaken
shine	shone	shone
shoot	shot	shot
show	showed	shown/-ed
shut	shut	shut
sing	sang	sung
sink	sank	sunk
sit	sat	sat
sleep	slept	slept
smell	smelt/-ed	smelt/-led
speak	spoke	spoken
spell	spelt/-ed	spelt/-led
spend	spent	spent
spill	spilt/-ed	spilt/-led
split	split	split
spring	sprang	sprung
stand	stood	stood
steal	stole	stolen
swim	swam	swum
take	took	taken
teach	taught	taught
tear	tore	torn
tell	told	told
think	thought	thought
throw	threw	thrown
understand	understood	understood
wake	woke	woken
wear	wore	worn
win	won	won
write	wrote	written